THE OFFICIAL

THE
Get 'Em Girl's
GUIDE
TO UNLOCKING
THE **POWER** OF
Cuisine

BY Shakara Bridgers, Jeniece Isley, AND Joan Davis

RECIPE CONSULTANT Therese Nelson

Subira Publishing

THE Get 'Em Girl's GUIDE
TO UNLOCKING THE POWER OF CUISINE

Subira Publishing
P.O. Box 3384
New York, NY 10163
www.subirapublishing.com

Subira Publishing

For information about special discounts for bulk purchases, please contact Subira Publishing Special Sales: 1-877-699-1969 or business@subirapublishing.com

Book Cover Illustration by Jennifer Cruté

Photography by Terrell Belin

Book Cover & Layout Design by Kerry DeBruce

Editing by Wendy Catalano

Library of Congress Cataloging-in-Publication Data
has been applied for.
ISBN-13: 978-0-9791832-0-1
ISBN-10: 0-9791832-0-0
Printed in the United States of America

10 9 8 7 6 5 4 3 2 1

First Edition

Table of Contents

This book is dedicated to our Mommies: Deirdre, Jennifer, and Sandra.

Acknowledgements

Jeniece — **Thank you Lord,** for allowing me to see this dream come to fruition. God knows I fall short, and yet you still continue to bless me!

Mommy— The best cook in the WORLD, for as long as I can remember, you have supported each and every one of my dreams; for that I thank you! I love you so much—you're the best! **Daddy**— I love you, and I know you are smiling on me. **Crystal**— You know you like my cooking, so stop fronting! Thank you for being the best sister a girl can ask for. **Kayla**— The world is a better place with you in it! You are the most talented and beautiful little girl I know; I couldn't have asked for a better niece. **Dee**— What can I say? You are my muse; thank you for letting me experiment on you. You will be my taste-tester forever—you are stuck with me! I love you, baby. **Shakara**— My business partner and best friend, you truly love hard girl, but I'm riding with you…all the way to Oprah! **Joan**— Thank you for being the balance, the voice of reason, the referee, and the confidante between Shakara and me. **Amithy**— thank you for being the best friend a girl could ask for—and for blessing me with two beautiful godchildren. **Shanya** and **Justin**— I love you! **Nazae**— I'm a deadbeat godmommy, but I love you still! I'm going to get it right—I promise! **Danni**— We go through it, but I appreciate your friendship—you've put up with me for this long, I guess forever won't be so bad!

To the rest of my family: O-Mac— You are the most positive and hungry black man I've ever met…and I love you to death. **Rashein** and **Madisyn**— Love you! The entire **Isley Family**— Love you. **Dorian**— Continue to be the Lil' Diva that you are. **Bertina** and **Charlay**— Love you!

To my friends: Pretty K— From first grade to infinity! **Kirsten**, the make-up diva— Let's eat! **Badu**— Thank you for your encouragement… **Khalil**— Thanks for continuing to believe…now if only you'd get right, we could get you married! **Leah**— You are crazy as hell, but I can't imagine how I'd spend my days at work without you. **Dwayne**— "Much like the letter that Paul wrote to the Corinthians…" thank you for the love and ALWAYS keeping it real! **PV**— Stay sweet. **Nancy**— Thank you for the advice and the beauty tips— is it prunes and moisturizer that keep you looking fabulous? **Russ**— Thank you for the support! **Guy**— You sent the first check in—so you know I got you! **Artie**, **Ernest**, and **Jose**— Thank you for always looking out for me!

To the ladies of KLAD Creative, **Kerry** and **Leslie**— Thank you for jumping right in on this project and helping bring it to life—you two are the best! **Jennifer Cruté, illustrator extraordinaire**— Thank you for restoring our faith. You came right in and made it happen. **Terrell Belin**— You are a bad man—Thank you for all you do. **Wendy Catalano**— Thank you. **Therese Nelson**— You are the best at what you do. I wish you all the success in the world, and I want to be right there when you make your television debut! **Traci**— You did an amazing job!

Joan — **God**, you did it once again for me; Father I thank you for providing everything we needed to make this all possible. **My heartfelt thanks are extended to everyone** who supported me through this process with prayers and encouraging words; I thank you and send you my most sincere gratitude. I am forever indebted to the people who have inspired and molded me into the woman that I am today.

My love and thanks go out to my mom, who continuously believes in me, supports me, and challenges me to achieve greatness. Mommy, you are wonderful and I thank God for you daily. **To my late grandmother, Lilly Davis-Scott**— I know you are smiling down on me. **Aunt Tiny**— All your hard work has paid off; thanks for your love, patience, and recipes. **Jimetta and the boys**— Thanks for everything. **Swathavia**— You are the best; your humor has gotten me through many days. **The entire Davis family**— You guys are so very special to me. It's because of you that I work as hard as I do.

Shakia Monique Knight— Thank you for seventeen years of friendship; your listening ear even from across the world means a lot to me, and I don't take it for granted. A very special thanks to **Pastor McCann** and **Mrs. McCann** who have instilled an immeasurable number of wisdom pearls into my life, and to the **St. Luke Nation**— Kin-Dom Achievers; may God shift you to greater heights as you move from vision to fruition. **Ms. Cookie**— Keep doing what you do, darling; you have supported us 100 percent and I'm truly grateful. **Jeniece**— Without a doubt, you are one of the most gifted women in this world; I have so much respect for you. **Shakara Bridgers**— Wow, I have never met anyone as passionate about hip-hop as you. I know you'll be there for me if I ever need you! **Yvette Fonéy**— You are a wonderful person and I thank God for blessing me with your friendship. **The Lynch Family, Tyson, Leslie Smalls, Deidrea McIntosh, Julia Baker, Steve Wright, Keith Reed, my "Gain and Loss Crew", my friends in the Operating Room** and at **East Side Tab**— You guys are simply the best and I love you! **Terrell Belin** of Belin Photography - This is only the beginning; the best is yet to come for you! **Kerry DeBruce, Jennifer Crute** and **Wendy Catalano** - God sent you guys to us right in the nick of time.

Shakara — **God**— Thanks for your guidance; through you, all things are possible.

For so long I made up excuses as to why I didn't know how to cook, I feel so liberated now that I can!

Mommy— Thanks for always supporting me. You are my best friend. I am truly blessed to be your child. **Daddy**— I love you more than you know…more than I show. **Tanitsha**— I wouldn't trade you in for the world. You're my only sister, I love you. **Grandma**— You have always believed in me. You are so sweet and kind. It is my desire to be successful so that I can spoil you. **Great Grandma Beulah**— It's amazing how beautiful you still look at ninety! **Hilton**— Being a stepfather isn't always easy, but you make it seem effortless.

Aunt Renee, Aunt Andrea, Aunt Sharon, Aunt Joyce, Aunt Ann, Uncle Michael, Uncle Ricky, and Uncle James— Thanks for always looking out for me. Your guidance has helped me grow into a responsible woman. I love you all. **Andrenique & Cochise**— Hold tight. Your oldest cousin has got your back. **Damon**— I miss you. **Leonard**— Follow your dreams and you will always be successful. To the **Bridgers, Brown, Sherrod** and **Mills** families— I love you all, and thanks for being there for me throughout the years. **Jamal, CJ, Shannon, Steven, Cathy, Michelle, LaJohn, Mia, Ursula** and **Emika**— Thanks for being great cousins.

Moms— You are truly a rider. You have supported Jeniece, Joan, and me from day one. You have sacrificed so much for our success. Thanks for loving me as if I were your own.

Joan— Your passion for God moves me. You are a gentle person. Thanks for being my business partner and friend. **Jeniece**— What can I say? You are my friend for life. You are so talented; I have never seen you fail. I feed off of your energy— it inspires me. I couldn't ask for a better business partner. **Satarah "Tori"**— You are my twin from another mother. It is not too often that you find someone you get along with all of the time. You are so strong and beautiful. I could not have made it through college without you. **Resonda**— Thanks for making me a godmother. I am so proud of you and Bunny. LB and Nakia Janee are so beautiful. **Tasha**— Girl, you are my heart. Just remember, I am here if you need me. **Crystal**— Slow down! I can never catch up with you.

LB, **Nakia Janee**, **Morgan**, **Yalaina**, **Briana**, **Curtis**, **Corey**, **Javon**, **Davon**, **Rasheed**, **Rashad**, **Sydney**, **Sierra**, and **Kayla**— You are the next generation. Enjoy being young! Listen to your parents and don't take any wooden nickels. I love all of you; call on me if you need me.

Peter "Guttaperk"— Thanks for always looking out for me. We have made money together and we have lost money together; throughout all of this we have remained friends.

Leah & Valerie— Thanks for being my friends. It is not too often that coworkers form true friendships. There will always be a job for you at Subira Publishing…lol!

Thanks to all of my friends who have supported me— **Jango, CL, Dee, Dwayne, Troy Marshall, Shawn "Tubby" Holiday, Gary, Ed, Cedric, Jeremy, Lavel, Beverly, Kyjuan, Ash, Amithy, Adri, Abdul, Benji, Damian (Brotha), Phoenix, Will, Deangelo, Delroy, Dirty, Dino, Donna, Koren, Kirsten, Tracy, Ellen, Jermaine, Tamir, Kim, Kandece, Don & Sasha Baker, Lena, Lisa, Marcus & Natasha Kelly, Johnny "NuBuzz" Nunez, Mark, Vonnie, Veronica, JB, Spencer, Olympia, Tay, Mary Rose, Linda, Elva, Dr. Sean P. Gardner, Sr. & The Eastward Baptist Church.**

Thanks to **Kerry, Leslie, Terrell, Wendy, Therese, Jennifer** and **Jackie O.** for seeing our vision and helping us create this beautiful book.

Jerry— I look forward to building a future with you. You make me feel like the most beautiful girl in the world. I love you.

The Get 'Em Girl's Points to Remember

*I*f you're reading this, you have purchased this cookbook or are thinking about purchasing it. For that we thank you! When we decided to write this book we knew that we would get some strong supporters and some even stronger detractors. We just want to let you know that this book in no way, shape, or form, is meant to marginalize women. Our goal is to uplift women, to give them options. Dating is hard! We've tried everything else; why not try something that everyone can benefit from?

1. YOU CAN'T GET WHAT DOESN'T WANT TO BE GOTTEN!
Simply put, you can bake a peach cobbler that will bring tears to his eyes, but if he's not ready to be in a relationship, it is an exercise in futility. If you find that your efforts are constantly in vain and unappreciated, pick up your apron, dust the flour off your shoulders, and keep it moving.

2. YOU HAVE TO SIMMER BEFORE YOU BOIL! Don't start with filet mignon and try to bring him back down to Steak-Ums—it won't work. Start slowly and pace yourself!

3. DON'T START WHAT YOU CAN'T FINISH! Ladies, if you start out cooking seven days a week, he will expect you to cook seven days a week. Be as realistic as possible when making the decision to cook for your potential love. This will save you the trouble of trying to break him out of daily dinners when, and if, he becomes your man.

Are you ready ladies? Let's go get 'em!

Introduction

Get 'Em Girl: An ambitious woman who uses unconventional ways to achieve her goals.

*W*hen we first decided to write this book, it was based solely on our love of three things: food, fun, and men! Being three single women living in New York City, we knew all too well, the pitfalls of dating in the big city. Young and career-oriented, we didn't have a real need (or want) to cook. Yes, we had to eat, but this is New York! There is a restaurant, deli, or take-out place on every other block. However, we also knew that to date (and keep) a man in a place as big as New York, which is full of beautiful women of all backgrounds, we had to step the game up. We had to sit back and ask ourselves, What are we bringing to the table? Yes, we all are beautiful, intelligent, and educated—but so are the tens of thousands of other women waiting to take our places. So instead of trying to decipher what men want in a woman, we just asked them.

We set out with our list of questions and hit the streets (well actually, the barbershops, supermarkets, churches, workplaces, and chat rooms) with one goal in mind: to find out what it is that men really want. While some definitely didn't want much (all you have to do is know how to drop it like it's hot and pick it up slow) almost all of them asked the inevitable, "…but can you cook?"

Now we have all heard the saying "The way to a man's heart is through his stomach," and most of us probably think it's an old-fashioned cliché that doesn't fit in this day and age. But as sure as the day is long, it's just as relevant today, if not more so, as it was fifty years ago. Contrary to how fine you know you are, a man is turned on by any woman who is willing to invest the slightest bit of time and energy in pleasing him.

The purpose of this book is not to have women chained to the stove, but to re-introduce women to the art form of cooking, which if done properly, can be easy, fun, and delicious. Just think about it, if you met a man at his place for a quiet evening, just to get to know each other, and found yourself presented with herb-roasted chicken, sautéed broccolini, and mushroom rice pilaf, you would be liable to lose all your religion and good sense—well after you ate, of course. Aside from this being an immensely thoughtful thing to do, the fact that he dedicated the time to cook such an elaborate meal for you would probably send you right over the edge. Well, the same goes for him.

So with that said, if he's worth it, and if you're playing for keeps, impress him with that little thing you do with your tongue—and that little thing you do with your skillet.

10 Reasons to Cook for Your Man

1 **YOU WILL HAVE ONE MORE THING TO IMPRESS HIM WITH.** Of course he's turned on by your beautiful smile and sense of humor, but why not show him your other talents?

2 **TO ADD A LITTLE VARIETY TO AN OTHERWISE BORING MEAL.** Take him to the Caribbean on Tuesday and back to the Carolinas on Wednesday. Change is good— especially when it's good food!

3 **BECAUSE YOU ARE A SHOW OFF!** There is nothing wrong with tooting your own horn; hell, if you don't do it, no one will. Show him that you're out of the ordinary!

4 **COOKING CAN BE FUN AND FLIRTATIOUS!** Try wearing a very sexy outfit and heels while you serve him and watch how he responds to you.

5 **YOU HAVE TO EAT TOO!** We know it sounds basic, but it's the truth. You can save a lot of money by cooking your own dinner and taking leftovers to work. No matter why you choose to cook, it's a win/win situation for you.

6 **WE'RE SURE YOU CAN FIND BETTER THINGS TO DO WITH THE MONEY SPENT DINING OUT EVERY NIGHT.** Eating out every now and then is cool; however, eating out daily can be expensive and mundane. Don't let your man get too accustomed to other people serving him.

7 **HOW ELSE CAN HE GIVE THAT STAR-STUDDED PERFORMANCE THAT YOU ARE ACCUSTOMED TO?** Just like a car can't run without fuel, neither can your man. If you expect mind blowing performances then make sure you give him the nourishment he needs to step up to the plate.

8 **HE DESERVES IT.** You realize you've got a keeper – show him how much he is appreciated.

9 **YOU LOVE HIM WAY MORE THAN THE DELIVERY GUY.** Aside from quickly becoming boring and expensive, take-out is the easy way out and should always be the last resort.

10 **LAST BUT NOT LEAST – YOU ARE A** Get 'Em Girl!
No explanation needed!

Plan of Action

*I*f the thought of cooking is frightening to you, we are here to tell you not to fret. Not everyone has the innate knowledge of how to cook—some of us chose to sit and watch our parents, while the rest of us picked up every book we could find on how to re-create our favorite dishes. No matter what method you choose to follow when getting your feet wet in the kitchen, there are some basics guidelines to stocking up and being prepared.

FIRST AND FOREMOST

Before you begin, make sure you read each recipe and menu thoroughly. This will help you to get acquainted with the ingredients, tools needed, and recipe steps.

TAKE STOCK

Making sure that you always have the basic staples to whip up the perfect "in-no-time" meal is key. You will save yourself a world of headaches by always keeping a few key ingredients in stock. For instance, canned beans, tomato sauce, chili powder, and ground cumin can be whipped up in an instant –into a hearty vegetarian chili!

TAKE SHORTCUTS WHEN NECESSARY

Although the premise of this book is about going back to basics, we are realists – and realistically, there are times when shortcuts just make better sense. For instance, store-bought marinara sauces work in a pinch. Yes, making your own sauce is ideal, but sometimes time just doesn't permit. Also, pre-cut veggies are perfect to have in the freezer, just in case. Use your best judgment when taking shortcuts and you will be fine.

QUALITY OVER QUANTITY

Remember, you are preparing an intimate dinner for your potential mate, not a smorgasbord. Keep it simple and easy. You will find that three well thought-out and creative dishes are worth more than ten thrown-together meals any day. Don't overwhelm yourself by trying to make every dinner a Thanksgiving meal. Before you know it, you'll be worn out and back to drive-through windows. Pace yourself!

MAKING SUBSTITUTIONS

If you see a recipe that you just absolutely have to try, but you are watching your calories, carbohydrates, or fat intake, try substituting some of the ingredients for their reduced-fat alternatives. It's really up to your taste —just play with it. You may have to adjust the seasoning, and the consistency of some of the dishes, but let your taste buds be the judge.

WHEN ALL ELSE FAILS, GO WITH WHAT YOU KNOW!

Rome wasn't built in a day, and your cooking skills won't be either. If you are pressed for time or if you are trying to make a big impression, stick to the basics.

Taking Stock

*N*ow that you've made the decision to cook for the man you are so crazy about, the last thing you need is for him to be on his way with expectations of a fabulous meal when you realize you have no curry for your Curried Chicken and Rice. Here is a list of staples that should be on hand in your refrigerator and pantry. Whether you want to whip up a quick meal for yourself or a little something for your man, you can choose which ingredients best fit your style of cooking.

ASIAN SEASONINGS: soy sauce, teriyaki sauce, oyster sauce, hoisin sauce

BAKING NEEDS: double-acting baking powder, baking soda, extracts (vanilla, almond, lemon, etc.), flour (all-purpose, cake and self-rising)

BEANS AND LEGUMES: any type of canned and dried varieties that you like

BROTH AND STOCKS: chicken, vegetable, and/or beef

BUTTER: salted and unsalted

CARIBBEAN SEASONINGS: jerk seasoning, curry powder, browning, coconut milk

CHEESES: Parmigiano-Reggiano (shredded, cubed or wedge), and any other varieties you like

CONDIMENTS: mayonnaise, prepared mustard (Dijon and yellow), salsa, ketchup, hot pepper sauce, honey

EGGS: large, farm-fresh

FRUIT: lemons, limes, and/or oranges

GARLIC: whole, and chopped in olive oil

GRAINS: ground cornmeal, rice (brown, basmati, long-grain, etc.), oatmeal

HERBS (DRIED): oregano, thyme, rosemary, Italian seasoning blend

HERBS (FRESH): basil, Italian flat-leaf parsley, mint, thyme, rosemary

MILK: condensed, evaporated, whole (or low/no-fat)

NUTS: walnuts, pecans, and/or almonds

OIL: extra virgin olive oil, vegetable oil, peanut oil

ONIONS: red and yellow onions, shallots, scallions

PASTA: long (fettuccine, spaghetti, etc.) and short (rotini, macaroni, penne, etc.)

POTATOES: red bliss, russet, and/or Yukon

SEAFOOD (CANNED): tuna and salmon

SPICES: cinnamon, chili powder, bay leaves, nutmeg, salt (kosher, iodized, seasoned), pepper (whole black pepper, white pepper, and cayenne), seasoning blends (seafood and/or steak seasoning)

SUGARS: brown, granulated refined, confectioners'

TOMATOES (CANNED): whole, crushed, paste

VINEGARS: balsamic, red wine, white

Equipment Check

*Y*ou fight your way through the hustle and bustle of midtown traffic to get to your favorite department store—on a Wednesday, no less. You make your way to the "Cellar" and immediately get the chills. You realize just then that you've stepped into kitchen utopia and have absolutely no idea what you're looking for. Step to the side, let the other shoppers off the escalator, and take three deep breaths—feel better? Okay, let's get started. Ideally, you want heavy-bottomed pots and pans that are made of stainless steel—preferably with copper bottoms (copper conducts heat better than stainless steel, although they do require frequent polishing). The handles should be riveted to the pan and oven-safe—don't forget the lids.

SMALL SAUCEPAN: holds approximately two quarts and is good for melting butter, warming milk, and re-heating sauces.

MEDIUM SAUCEPAN: holds about four quarts and is great for making pasta sauces, rice, and small portions of soup.

LARGE STOCKPOT: holds about eight quarts and is ideal for cooking pasta, soups, and stews.

SMALL SKILLET: for making omelets and toasting nuts.

MEDIUM SKILLET: for stir-frying and sautéing. Consider getting a cast-iron skillet as well, for frying and browning.

LARGE SKILLET (OPTIONAL): great for large dishes like paella.

ROASTING PAN: a must-have for slow roasting.

GRILL PAN: just the right tool for indoor picnics.

---

*I*f you intend on baking, here are a few basic essentials needed.

ROUND CAKE PANS, THREE 9-INCH, WITH STRAIGHT SIDES: you'll need these for that Red Velvet Cake you plan on making to go with that red velvet teddy you plan on wearing.

COOKIE SHEETS: everybody loves cookies, and you can't make them in a skillet.

SPRINGFORM: Pan, 9- or 10-inch: ideal for making cheesecakes and tortes.

MUFFIN TIN, 12-CUP: well, for muffins.

COOLING RACKS: just what you need to allow your baked goods to cool evenly.

ASSORTED MIXING BOWLS: useful for prepping for your baking projects as well as mixing batters.

MEASURING CUPS AND SPOONS: it's all about precision and exact measurements with baking, so make sure you have the right tools.

---

*Y*ou made it through cookware and bakeware and your hands are almost full, but you can't leave without knives. When you set out to get a knife set you will probably be surprised at the range of prices and quality. The old adage "you get what you pay for" has never been more true than when you are shopping for knives. Be sure to purchase knives with high-carbon stainless steel blades. The handles should be riveted to the blade and they should feel slightly heavy and evenly weighted in your hand.

CHEF'S KNIFE: 8- or 10-Inch: personally, we are 10-inch girls, but purchase whichever is comfortable for you. Ideal for cutting meat and vegetables.

PARING KNIFE: has a 3-inch blade and is great for peeling and cutting fruits and vegetables.

SERRATED KNIFE: great for slicing crusty bread loaves.

STEAK KNIVES (OPTIONAL): if you plan on making steak, these will come in handy—we promise.

SHARPENING STEEL: sharpens and realigns your knives.

You may want to grab a cart for the next section—appliances and gadgets, baby! There are so many kitchen gadgets and appliances to choose from; they do everything from spin salads to peel potatoes. For now, keep it basic and use your better judgment when choosing which products are essential and which are just plain ridiculous. Here are a few that we think are essential to everyday cooking.

FOOD PROCESSOR: durable and useful for everything from mixing pastry dough to grating cheese. You will wonder how you made it this far without one.

BLENDER: great for smoothies, daiquiris, margaritas, daiquiris, coladas, oh— and daiquiris.

ELECTRIC MIXER: choose a stand or hand mixer; whichever your budget permits.

CUTTING BOARD: plastic boards are easier to clean and take care of but wood boards are so damn sexy! Periodically rub them down with mineral oil (we're still talking about cutting boards, freshy!) to keep them from cracking.

COLANDER: essential for draining pasta and washing vegetables.

---

*M*ore **Appliances and Gadgets:**
The following gadgets are also essential to everyday cooking;

PEPPER MILL	**VEGETABLE PEELER**
WINE RACK	**WOODEN SPOONS**
WHISK	**SLOTTED SPOON**
SLOTTED SPATULA	**CHEESE GRATER**
RUBBER SPATULA	**THERMOMETER**
LADLE	**KITCHEN-GRADE FIRE EXTINGUISHER**
PINCER-TYPE TONGS	

Is He Worth It?

*T*he day is here. You finally worked up the nerve to ask the handsome man you keep bumping into at the cleaners out for drinks, and it was a success! After weeks of restaurant hopping and movie dates you decide you want to invite him over for a nice home-cooked meal. Before you run out and spend your entire check at Whole Foods, or purchase that candy red KitchenAid mixer, ask yourself—is he worth it?

We understand he's cute and his body is to die for, but would he appreciate you sweating out your fresh 'do shucking oysters for homemade Oyster Bisque? (Okay—so you won't be shucking the oysters; you can leave that to your fish monger, but he doesn't know that) If the answer is yes, then call your hairdresser for an appointment and get in that kitchen! If you're not too sure, just ask yourself the following questions:

WAS THERE A CONNECTION? Can you see yourself being in a quiet place with this man for hours, and not running out of things to talk about? Or did you find yourself sending S.O.S. text messages to your girlfriends to come save you from this hell called a date?

CAN HE HOLD A CONVERSATION? Did he keep your attention? Was he a good listener? Was he engaging or evasive?

WAS HE RESPECTFUL? Did he come to your door and pick you up for the date or did he call you from his car and tell you to be outside in 5 minutes? Did he damn near break his neck when the cute waitress walked by?

DOES HE HAVE A SENSE OF HUMOR? Were you laughing at his jokes to spare his feelings? For one minute, did you wish Sandman Sims was around to pull his behind out of the restaurant?

DID HE ARRIVE WITH DRAMA? Was the baggage he brought to the table Ziploc® or garbage bag sized? When talking about his ex, did his left eye twitch unconsciously?

IS HE INSECURE? Did you have to hear about his days as a semi-pro baller over and over? Was he trying too hard to impress you with stories about his famous ex-girlfriend?

Table 101

*t*here comes a time in a woman's life when TV tables will not do. This is one of those times. We are trying to make a lasting impression on the man that just may be your future, so pack up the Dixie cups, push the paper plates to the back of the cupboard, and break out the matching service for four that you got as a housewarming gift.

SETTING THE TABLE If your dining table is a hand-me-down disaster, an occasional-table moonlighting as a dinette set, or if you just want to protect the furniture that you worked hard for, you may want to start with a tablecloth. They are simple enough to purchase; just hit up Linens 'N Things or Target. They come in so many cool styles and colors, just make sure you get the right shape and length for your table – and don't forget to iron it! Next, pick up a set of cloth napkins. Ideally, they should match or coordinate with your tablecloth. But if your own personal style dictates striped tablecloth and paisley napkins—do you! Napkin rings are a classy touch to the table setting, though definitely not necessary. If you're taking him on a Trip for Two to the Caribbean, tie a piece of natural raffia around the napkins for a cute (and cheap) play on your dinner's theme.

LIGHT IT UP! Head over to Yankee Candle and pick up some pillar or tea light candles to create a mood-enhancing centerpiece. But don't get too candle crazy—shimmying down the fire escape in your 4-inch Giuseppe Zanotti's isn't sexy.

DISHES, GLASSES, SILVERWARE—OH MY! Once again, they should all match. Simple white plates are perfectly fine, and get some Oneida in your life and pick up a set of matching flatware as well. A set of wine glasses might set you back about fifty-two cents at Ikea, so get a couple of sets. But if you want glasses that can withstand more than four cycles in the dishwasher you may want to pay a little more. Either way, make sure they match.

The illustration shown is a table setting for a casual dinner. There are more than a few ways to set a table, from basic to "this is ridiculous." We don't have enough table space for "this is ridiculous," so here you go. *(smile)*

1. Wine, water, or pineapple juice—whichever you prefer, the glass goes over the dinner knife.

2. Dinner plate should be placed in the center.

3. Remember those cloth napkins we mentioned earlier? Well this is where they go, whether neatly folded into a rectangle or with a napkin ring.

4. Salad anyone? This is the fork for it.

5. Set the dinner fork directly to the left of the plate—please?

6. Knives should be placed to the right of the plate with the cutting edge facing the dinner plate.

7. The spoon goes to the far right—yes, right there.

Wasn't that easy? All right, now that we have the table in order, let's work on the wine selection. Come on, you can do it!

Wine Basics

Selecting the right wine to complement your meal can be a harrowing experience for a beginner, but a little knowledge can minimize the intimidation factor. In fact, wine choice should be based on what you like, first and foremost. To help you select the wine that best complements the meal you are preparing, there are some basic principals to go by. Generally, white wines go well with delicately flavored foods, while red wines often pair better with heartier meals. Ultimately, the decision is yours to make and should always be based on your personal taste.

Below, we put together a list of popular whites and reds to help in choosing the perfect wine for your evening:

WHITE WINES:

CHABLIS *(Sha-blee)*
How does it taste: Refreshing but not overwhelming.
Pairs well with: Seafood, poultry, and salads with non-acidic dressing.

CHARDONNAY *(Shar-doe-nay)*
How does it taste: Generally, chardonnays can range in flavor from the light and crisp apple-like flavor of those from France, to Australian chardonnays which have aromas of tropical fruit and honey.
Pairs well with: Pasta, shrimp, poultry, and mild fish varieties for the lighter wines; and pork, salmon, and tuna for the heavier varieties.

GEWURZTRAMINER *(Geh-vertz-trah-mee-nur)*
How does it taste: Floral with aromas of nutmeg and cloves.
Pairs well with: Spicy, Asian dishes go very well with the crisp varieties, while the sweeter varieties are best served with cheese or dessert.

PINOT GRIGIO/GRIS *(Pee- noe Gree-joe/Gree)*
How does it taste: Pinot Grigio has a subtle taste, while Pinot Gris has a fruitier flavor.
Pairs well with: Roasted chicken or pork, shellfish, and eggs—especially omelets.

RIESLING *(Reese-ling)*
How does it taste: Has a well-balanced and subtle flavor of honey and fruit, which vary from dry to very sweet, depending on the origin and time of harvest.
Pairs well with: Steamed fish and spicy foods. Late-harvest varieties are good as a dessert wine.

SAUVIGNON BLANC *(So-veen-yawn Blahn)*
How does it taste: Dry, tart flavor with notes of citrus, melon, and passion fruit.
Pairs well with: Grilled seafood, poultry, vegetables, and spicy foods.

RED WINES

BOURDEAUX *(Bore-DOH)*
How does it taste: Fruity and light- to medium-bodied, or rich, complex, and full-bodied.
Pairs well with: Roasted red meats and chicken as well as spicy pasta.

CABERNET SAUVIGNON *(Cab-air-nay So-veen-yawn)*
How does it taste: Oaky, with a hint of blackberry, plum, and black cherry.
Pairs well with: Roasted or grilled red meats, turkey, and chicken.

CHIANTI *(Ki-ahn-tee)*
How does it taste: Light and easy wine with the taste of berries and hints of spice.
Pairs well with: Pizza, pasta, roasted chicken or fish, and steak.

RED WINES *(continued)*

PINOT NOIR *(Pee-noe Nwahr)*
How does it taste: Fruity, with hints of cherry, plum, and pepper.
Pairs well with: Chicken, pork, lamb, and salmon.

RIOJA *(Ree-oh-hah)*
How does it taste: Fruity flavor of berries and plums with a hint of vanilla and spice.
Pairs well with: Mildly spicy Latin and Asian dishes as well as roasted meat, chicken, salmon, and tuna.

SANGIOVESE *(Sahn-joe-vay-zeh)*
How does it taste: Spicy with hints of cherries, raspberries, and anise.
Pairs well with: Pasta, fish, seafood, and roasted meats.

SHIRAZ/SYRAH *(Shee-rahz/See-rah)*
How does it taste: Ripe and fruity, with a subtle spiciness.
Pairs well with: Pizza, chili, and roasted salmon.

ZINFANDEL *(Zin-fahn-dell)*
How does it taste: Bright and spicy with a hint of plums, raspberries, or blackberries.
Pairs well with: Prime rib, sausages, chicken wings, and stews.

It's Not *His Mama's...* But It *Comes Close*

Shakara's MENU

SIMPLE SOUTHERN FRIED CHICKEN

BAKED MACARONI AND CHEESE

LUSCIOUS CANDIED SWEETS

FRESH STRING BEANS AND RED POTATOES

STICKY MONKEY BREAD

SOUTHERN GIRL SWEET TEA

Jeniece's MENU

SO SERIOUS SUFFOCATED PORK CHOPS

BUTTERY RICE

COLLARD GREENS WITH SMOKED TURKEY WINGS

SWEET POTATO BISCUITS

SIMPLE AND SINFUL BANANA PUDDING

Joan's MENU

FRIED CATFISH FILETS

NOT HIS MAMA'S POTATO SALAD

FRIED CABBAGE AND BACON

SOUTHERN FRIED OKRA

SIMPLY SWEET CORNBREAD

RED VELVET CAKE

> I still don't know any woman who can cook better than my man
> and if I ever meet one I wouldn't tell her because
> I'd be giving her too much POWER,
>
> -JOSÉ MORENO *New York, NY*

*Y*ou know how great a cook you are. People have been telling you for years that you could put more than a few "soul food" restaurants out of business if they tasted your Blackberry Peach Cobbler. So the thought of your man coming over for a nice down-home dinner is a welcome challenge. In fact, you've been reading cookbooks all day to get just the right recipes down pat for your dinner with your baby, and when he gets there you know—wait, let's say that again— you KNOW he's going to lose his mind over the meal you have planned for him.

You have been burning in the kitchen all day. You've got the greens and smoked turkey wings on simmer, the chicken frying to a golden crisp, and the macaroni and cheese bubbling in the oven. When you bring your man his plate you wait until he takes the first bite, and you eagerly ask, "How does it taste?" After all your hard work, what is his answer?... "It's not my mama's, but it's good!" Ladies, I know at this point you want to snatch your plate back from his hands and go off on him, but don't! Contrary to the way it sounds, this is a compliment and one that should be regarded highly.

You see, even the slightest comparison of your cooking to his mother's, is a good thing. Consider this: When you think of your mom's cooking, aside from the taste, you probably think about memories that are some of the most enjoyable times of your life. Well, the same goes for him.

So the next time you bring him his plate and he looks up at you and makes that comparison, know that what he is actually saying to you is, "Are you trying to make me fall in love with you?" Smile slyly, and whisper softly... **Get 'Em Girl**

Simple *Southern* Fried Chicken

*t*here is absolutely nothing like good fried chicken. You will love the crispy coating of this chicken. Serve with a cold glass of Southern Girl's Sweet Tea. If it's a REALLY good evening serve him the leftovers, if there are any, with homemade buttermilk waffles the next morning. (SWEET TEA RECIPE ON PAGE 24 & WAFFLE RECIPE ON PAGE 53)

1 Clean and rinse chicken under cold water. Place in a container and add lemon juice, let sit for one minute and rinse well with cold water. Pat dry and season with 1-1/2 teaspoons salt and 1 teaspoon ground black pepper. Cover and refrigerate for at least 1 hour.

2 Place flour in a resealable plastic bag and season with salt and pepper.

3 Mix the eggs and the milk together in a wide, shallow bowl, and season with salt and pepper. Dip the chicken pieces into the egg mixture, and then place each piece in the bag. Shake until chicken is completely coated. Set aside while the oil is heating.

4 In a large skillet, preferably cast iron, heat oil over high heat until very hot, but not smoking, about 350 degrees. Carefully add chicken pieces, making sure not to overcrowd the skillet.

5 Fry chicken, uncovered, turning occasionally until golden brown on all sides and cooked throughout, about 6 minutes for breasts and wings, and 8 to 10 minutes for thighs and legs.

6 Remove the chicken from the skillet and drain on a paper towel-lined platter. Season with salt and pepper and serve immediately.
MAKES 4 SERVINGS

INGREDIENTS

1 chicken
(2-1/2 to 3 pounds),
cut into 8 pieces

1/2 cup lemon juice
(about 5 lemons)

Salt and ground black pepper

1-1/2 cups all-purpose flour

3 eggs

1/2 cup milk

Vegetable oil, for deep-frying

It's Not His Mama's... But It Comes Close

Baked *Macaroni* And *Cheese*

INGREDIENTS

1 pound (about 4 cups) elbow macaroni, uncooked

8 tablespoons, plus 2 tablespoons butter

1 cup shredded mild cheddar cheese

1 cup shredded sharp cheddar cheese

1/2 cup shredded Monterey Jack cheese

1 pint half-and-half

1 (12-ounce) can cheddar cheese soup
(recommended: Campbell's)

2 eggs, lightly beaten

1 teaspoon seasoned salt

1/2 teaspoon ground black pepper

*W*hile boxed Mac and Cheese may work if the man in your life just turned six, a grown man needs a little more. Layered with Monterey Jack, sharp and mild cheddar cheeses, this version is sure to bring back memories of Sunday dinners at his Mama's.

1 Preheat the oven to 350 degrees. Lightly butter a deep 2-1/2 quart casserole dish.

2 Bring a large pot of water to a boil over high heat. Stir in the elbow macaroni and cook until the macaroni is just tender, about 7 minutes. Do not overcook. Drain well and return to the pot.

3 Melt 8 tablespoons of butter in a small saucepan. Stir into the macaroni. In a large bowl, mix the mild and sharp Cheddar and Monterey Jack cheeses.

4 Stir into the macaroni, the half-and-half, 2 cups of the shredded cheese mixture, the can of cheddar cheese soup, and the eggs. Season with the seasoned salt and black pepper. Transfer to the buttered casserole. Sprinkle with the remaining 1/2 cup of shredded cheese and dot with the remaining 2 tablespoons of butter.

5 Bake until casserole begins to bubble around the edges, about 35 minutes.

MAKES 6 SERVINGS

MAKE IT YOUR OWN

Experiment with different cheeses. Add a 1/2 cup of asiago cheese for added bite, or substitute a 1/2 cup of pepper jack for the Monterey to add a little kick!

Luscious *Candied Sweets*

"i will never forget the first time I made these for my man; I think he fell in love with me the day I handed him his plate." *Jeniece*

1 Preheat the oven to 325 degrees. Lightly butter a 9 x 13-inch baking dish.

2 Bring a large pot of water to a boil over high heat. Thoroughly wash and scrub the sweet potatoes and add to the pot. Cook until tender, about 25 minutes. Drain and rinse under cold running water until cool enough to handle. Peel the sweet potatoes.

3 Combine the sugars, cinnamon, nutmeg, and allspice in a medium bowl. In a separate small bowl, combine the maple-flavored syrup and vanilla extract.

4 Slice the sweet potatoes into 1/2-inch thick rounds. Layer about half of the sweet potatoes in the prepared baking dish. Sprinkle with half of the sugar mixture and dot with 4 tablespoons of butter. Repeat with another layer of sweet potatoes and the remaining half of the sugar mixture, and dot with the remaining 4 tablespoons of butter. Top with the syrup mixture.

5 Basting occasionally with the syrup, bake for 35 to 45 minutes, or until the sweet potatoes are glazed. Serve hot.

MAKES 6 SERVINGS

TAKE NOTE

Contrary to what Sam your produce guy told you, yams and sweet potatoes are unrelated. In the U.S. the orange-flesh sweet potatoes are often mistakenly labeled as yams when in fact, yams are primarily black or brown-skinned and sold mostly in specialty markets that cater to Caribbean cuisine.

INGREDIENTS

8 medium unpeeled orange-flesh sweet potatoes

1/2 cup light brown sugar

1/2 cup granulated sugar

1/2 teaspoon cinnamon

1/2 teaspoon nutmeg

1/8 teaspoon allspice

1/2 cup maple-flavored syrup

1/2 teaspoon vanilla extract

8 tablespoons butter, softened

It's Not His Mama's... But It Comes Close

Fresh *Green Beans* With *Red Potatoes*

INGREDIENTS

1-1/2 pounds
fresh green beans

3 tablespoons olive oil

1 (1-pound) turkey wing

1 cup vegetable broth or water,
plus more if needed

1 teaspoon seasoned salt,
plus more to taste

1/4 teaspoon ground black
pepper, plus more to taste

1/4 teaspoon garlic powder

6 small unpeeled
red potatoes,
washed and scrubbed

1/4 cup onion, cut into slivers

2 tablespoons butter

*f*reeze! Step away from the can goods and head over to the produce aisle. Anyone can open up a can of watered-down veggies; why not impress your man by cooking fresh green beans?

1 Remove the ends from the green beans. Place the beans into a colander and rinse with cold water. Drain completely and set aside.

2 Heat the olive oil in a large Dutch oven, preferably cast iron, over medium heat. Add the turkey wing; cook and stir for about 8 minutes.

3 Toss the green beans into the pot, stirring them with a wooden spoon to coat well with oil. Stir in the broth, seasoned salt, pepper, and garlic powder. Cover tightly.

4 Cook over medium-low heat for about 25 minutes, or until the beans are half done.

5 Meanwhile, cut the potatoes in half and place in a bowl of cold water. At the end of the 25 minutes, add the potatoes and onions to the beans. Add 1/4 cup more broth, if needed.

6 Cover and continue to cook until the potatoes are tender, approximately 20 to 25 minutes, periodically checking the pot to make sure a small amount of liquid remains.

7 When the potatoes are tender, remove the lid. Continue to cook until the green beans are wilted, about 10 minutes. While cooking, stir in the butter and season with additional seasoned salt and pepper, if necessary.

MAKES 2 TO 4 SERVINGS

SAVE YOURSELF SOME TIME! If your supermarket has pre-snapped green beans, buy them! The expense isn't that much more, and you can spend the 20 to 30 minutes gained setting the stage for an unforgettable evening.

Sticky *Monkey* *Bread*

*i*f you don't have time to bake an apple pie or a chocolate cake, try this quick fix that will have him hanging from the ceiling and begging for more!

1 Preheat oven to 350 degrees. Spray a 12-cup fluted tube pan with nonstick cooking spray.

2 Mix the granulated sugar and cinnamon together in a medium bowl and set aside.

3 In a small saucepan over low heat, melt the butter and brown sugar, stirring well, and remove from heat. Sprinkle 1/2 cup of the walnuts into the bottom of the tube pan.

4 Toss the biscuits into the cinnamon-sugar mixture and set aside.

5 Layer half of the biscuits in the prepared tube pan, spoon half of the brown sugar mixture over the biscuits, and sprinkle with 1/2 cup of walnuts.

6 Repeat with the remaining biscuits, brown sugar mixture, and 1/2 cup of walnuts.

7 Bake for about 30 minutes. Let stand for 5 minutes. Place a plate on top and invert. Serve warm.

MAKES 8 SERVINGS

INGREDIENTS

1/2 cup granulated sugar

2 teaspoons cinnamon

1/2 cup (1 stick) butter

1/2 cup packed light brown sugar

1-1/2 cups chopped walnuts

2 (12-ounce) cans refrigerated biscuits

It's Not His Mama's... But It Comes Close

Southern Girl Sweet Tea

INGREDIENTS

6 orange pekoe tea bags
(recommended: Lipton or Luzianne)

1/8 teaspoon baking soda

2 cups boiling water

1-1/2 cups granulated sugar

6 cups cold water

Mint leaves, for garnish

Lemon wedges, for garnish

1 Place the teabags and baking soda in a large measuring cup. Pour the boiling water over the tea bags. Cover and steep for 15 minutes.

2 Remove the tea bags, do not squeeze. Pour the tea mixture into a 2-quart pitcher.

3 Stir in the sugar until completely dissolved. Add cold water; refrigerate until chilled. Garnish with mint leaves and lemon wedges. Serve over ice.

MAKES ABOUT 2 QUARTS

So-Serious Suffocated
Pork Chops

Caution! If you are not interested in having him show up at your house unannounced, with plate in hand, then these pork chops are NOT to be played with! Serve them with Buttery White Rice or Pure Bliss Mashed Potatoes and the two of you might as well find a warm blanket and a comfy spot on the couch — because he won't be going anywhere! Try this recipe with turkey chops for an equally delicious version.
(BUTTERY RICE RECIPE ON PAGE 26 & PURE BLISS MASHED POTATOES RECIPE ON PAGE 97)

1 In a large, heavy-bottom skillet, heat the vegetable oil over medium-high heat. Season both sides of the pork chops with 1 teaspoon seasoned salt and 1/2 teaspoon freshly ground black pepper.

2 Place 1/2 cup of all-purpose flour in a bowl and season to taste with seasoned salt and pepper. Dredge pork chops in flour, shaking off excess.

3 Using tongs, carefully add pork chops to the skillet. Cook until both sides are a golden brown, about 3 minutes per side. Transfer to a plate and cover loosely with aluminum foil to keep warm.

4 Pour off all but 1 tablespoon of oil, making sure not to pour off any of the flour bits at the bottom of the skillet. Reduce heat to medium and add the onion. Cook, stirring often until softened, about 3 minutes. Sprinkle the mixture with the remaining 2 tablespoons of flour and stir well.

5 Cook until flour begins to brown. Stir in the water and bring to a simmer. Season to taste with seasoned salt, pepper, and 1/4 teaspoon garlic powder.

6 Return the pork chops to the skillet. Reduce heat to medium-low and cover.

7 Cook, stirring occasionally, until the pork chops show no signs of pink when pierced at the bone, about 30 minutes.
MAKES 4 SERVINGS

INGREDIENTS

1/2 cup vegetable oil

4 center-cut, bone-in pork chops (about 8-ounces each)

Seasoned salt

Freshly ground black pepper

1/2 cup all-purpose flour, plus 2 tablespoons

1 medium onion, chopped

1/4 teaspoon garlic powder

1 cup cold water

It's Not His Mama's... But It Comes Close

Buttery Rice

INGREDIENTS

4 cups water

2 cups uncooked long-grain rice

4 tablespoons butter

1 teaspoon salt

1/2 teaspoon ground white pepper

1 In a medium saucepan, bring the water to a rapid boil over high heat. Add the rice, butter, salt and pepper. Reduce heat to low and cover tightly.

2 Simmer until the liquid is absorbed and the rice is tender, about 25 to 30 minutes. Remove from heat and let stand, covered, for 5 minutes. Fluff the rice with a fork and serve hot

MAKES 6 TO 8 SERVINGS

Collard Greens With Smoked Turkey Wings

*N*o Southern meal is complete without a tall glass of Lip-Puckering Lemonade and a side of good ole' collards. These mean greens will definitely bring him back for seconds, thirds, and fourths!

1 Bring 3 quarts of water to a boil in a large pot over medium-high heat. Stir in the smoked turkey wings, seasoned salt, black pepper, and hot pepper sauce. Reduce heat to medium; cover and cook until tender, about 1 hour.

2 In the meantime, wash collard greens thoroughly in a sink full of cold water. Lift greens out of the sink and transfer to a large bowl, allowing the grit to fall to the bottom of the sink. Repeat as necessary.

3 Remove the thick stem that runs down the center of the greens by holding the leaf in one hand and stripping the leaf down with the other. Stack 6 to 8 stripped leaves on top of each other, roll up, and slice into 1/2 to 1–inch thick slices.

4 Add the collard greens, sugar, and baking soda to the pot. Reduce heat to low, partially cover, and cook, stirring occasionally, just until greens are tender, about 30 to 45 minutes. Serve immediately with additional hot pepper sauce.

MAKES 4 SERVINGS

INGREDIENTS

2 smoked turkey wings, cut up

1 tablespoon seasoned salt

1-1/2 teaspoons freshly ground black pepper

1 teaspoon hot pepper sauce (optional)

3 bunches of collard greens

1-1/2 teaspoons sugar

1/8 teaspoon baking soda

Lip-Puckering Lemonade

1 In a large pitcher, combine the lemon juice and sugar, stirring continuously to dissolve the sugar. *2* Add the cold water and blend well. *3* Garnish with lemon wedges and serve over ice. **MAKES ABOUT 2 QUARTS**

INGREDIENTS

Juice of 8 large lemons, about 1 cup

1 cup granulated sugar, or to taste

7 cups cold water

Lemon wedges, for garnish

Ice cubes

It's Not His Mama's... But It Comes Close

Sweet Potato
Biscuits

INGREDIENTS

2 medium orange-flesh
sweet potatoes

1/4 cup sugar

1 large egg, beaten

1 tablespoon butter, melted

1 cup milk

3 cups self-rising flour

1 teaspoon baking powder

1/2 cup vegetable shortening

Who knew sweet potatoes were good for more than pies?

1 Preheat oven to 400 degrees.

2 Bring a large pot of water to a boil. Thoroughly wash and scrub the sweet potatoes and peel. Cut sweet potatoes into 1 1/2-inch chunks and add to the boiling water. Simmer for 20 minutes or until fork tender. Drain well and transfer to a large bowl. Mash with a potato masher and set aside to cool.

3 Beat the sugar, egg, and melted butter into the cooled, mashed sweet potatoes until smooth. Stir in milk and set aside.

4 In a separate bowl, sift together the flour and baking powder. Cut in shortening with a fork or pastry blender until mixture resembles small peas.

5 Make a well in the center of dry mixture. Stir in the sweet-potato mixture to make a soft dough.

6 Place the dough on a lightly floured work surface and knead gently, just until the surface of the dough isn't sticky, about 10 strokes.

7 Roll or pat dough into a 1/2-inch thick disk. Cut with a floured 2-1/2-inch biscuit cutter. Re-roll as necessary. Place biscuits 1 inch apart on an ungreased baking sheet.

8 Bake for 15 to 20 minutes or until the biscuits are lightly browned. Serve hot with butter.

MAKES 16 BISCUITS

Simple And *Sinful*
Banana Pudding

a classic dessert made super easy. Instant pudding teamed with sweetened condensed milk makes a perfect combination that saves you all the trouble of making homemade custard.

1 In a large bowl, blend pudding mix and milk with an electric mixer on low until the mixture begins to thicken, about 2 minutes. Blend in the condensed milk and vanilla extract until smooth.

2 With a plastic spatula, gently fold in the whipped topping.

3 Spread a small amount of the pudding mixture on the bottom of a trifle dish or glass bowl and cover with a layer of vanilla wafer cookies. Top with a layer of sliced bananas. Spoon 1/3 of the custard over bananas.

4 Continue layering cookies, bananas, and custard to make three layers of each, ending with custard. Cover with plastic wrap and chill until ready to serve.

MAKES 8 SERVINGS

INGREDIENTS

1 (3.4-ounce) package instant vanilla pudding mix

2 cups cold milk

1 (14-ounce) can sweetened condensed milk

1-1/2 teaspoons vanilla extract

1 (8-ounce) container frozen whipped topping, thawed

12 ripe bananas, sliced

1 (16-ounce) package vanilla wafer cookies

It's Not His Mama's... But It Comes Close

Fried *Catfish* *Fillets*

INGREDIENTS

Vegetable oil, for frying

4 catfish fillets
(about 4 ounces each),
skin removed

Seasoned salt

Salt and freshly ground
black pepper

2/3 cup milk

1 large egg

1 cup yellow cornmeal

1/2 cup all-purpose flour

Dash cayenne pepper

The key to good catfish is making sure the fish is as fresh as possible and the oil is the right temperature. This crunchy and light dish can be eaten as an appetizer or entrée.

1 Add about 3 inches of oil to a large, heavy skillet, preferably cast iron, and heat to 375 degrees.

2 Meanwhile, season both sides of the catfish fillets with 1 teaspoon seasoned salt and 1 teaspoon ground black pepper. Mix the milk and egg together in a wide, shallow bowl, and season to taste with seasoned salt and black pepper. In a separate bowl, mix the cornmeal, flour, and cayenne pepper. Season with additional seasoned salt and black pepper, to your taste.

3 Dip the catfish in the milk mixture and then dredge in the cornmeal mixture, making sure to cover the fillets completely. Carefully add the fish to the hot oil in batches so the pan is not over crowded.

4 Fry the fish for 3 to 5 minutes and then remove and drain on a paper towel-lined platter. Season immediately with a pinch of salt and ground black pepper. Serve hot with lemon wedges and hot pepper sauce.

MAKES 2 TO 4 SERVINGS

INGREDIENTS

5 cups Lip-Puckering
Lemonade (SEE RECIPE, PAGE 27)

4 cups Southern Girl's
Sweet Tea (SEE RECIPE, PAGE 24)

Lemon wedges, for garnish

Half-and-Half with Lemonade Ice Cubes

1 Fill an empty ice cube tray with 1 cup lemonade and freeze until solid *2* Transfer lemonade ices cubes to a large pitcher. Pour the tea and the remaining lemonade over the ice cubes and stir to blend. Garnish with lemon wedges and serve.

MAKES ABOUT 2 QUARTS

Not-His-Mama's
Potato Salad

*l*ike a hug from your man after a long day, there is something comforting about warm potato salad. Ok, it's not that serious—but this potato salad is GOOD!

1 Bring a large pot of water to a boil over high heat. Add the potatoes. Cook until tender, about 25 minutes. Drain and rinse under cold running water until cool enough to handle. Peel the potatoes and cut into medium-sized cubes.

2 Combine the potatoes, onions, pickle relish, and eggs in a large bowl.

3 Season potato mixture with seasoned salt, black pepper, onion powder, garlic powder, and sugar. In a separate bowl mix together the mayonnaise, mustard, and vinegar. With a plastic spatula or wooden spoon, gently fold the mayonnaise mixture into the potato mixture, making sure not to break up the potatoes. Cover and chill in the refrigerator for several hours before serving.

MAKES 4 TO 6 SERVINGS

TAKE NOTE

For hard-cooked eggs, place the eggs in a pot of cold water and bring to a full boil. Cover tightly and remove from heat. Let stand for 10 full minutes in the hot water – this will help to prevent that ugly yellow line that forms when eggs are over-boiled.

INGREDIENTS

4 to 6 large unpeeled Idaho potatoes, washed and scrubbed

1 small yellow onion, finely chopped

1/2 cup sweet pickle relish, drained

4 hard-cooked eggs (see below), chopped

2 teaspoons seasoned salt

1-1/2 teaspoons ground black pepper

1/2 teaspoon onion powder

1/4 teaspoon garlic powder

1 teaspoon granulated sugar

1-1/2 cups mayonnaise

2 tablespoons prepared yellow mustard

1 teaspoon white vinegar

It's Not His Mama's... But It Comes Close

Fried *Cabbage* And *Bacon*

INGREDIENTS

3 slices uncooked bacon

1 tablespoon butter

1 (2-1/2 to 3-pound) head of cabbage, washed and coarsely chopped

1/4 teaspoon seasoned salt

1/4 teaspoon ground black pepper

1/2 teaspoon granulated sugar

1/4 cup water

1/4 teaspoon white vinegar (optional)

1 Cook the bacon in a large pot over medium heat, until crisp. Remove the bacon from the pot. Crumble and set aside.

2 Add the butter to the pot. Carefully add the cabbage, stirring well to coat the leaves in the bacon and butter mixture. Add the remaining ingredients to the pot and cover with a tight-fitting lid. Cook over medium heat for about 10 to 15 minutes.

3 Remove the lid and scatter the crumbled bacon over the top of the cabbage. Cover and cook for an additional 3 to 5 minutes. Serve hot.

MAKES 4 TO 6 SERVINGS

Southern
Fried *Okra*

*a*lso known as "southern popcorn." Fry up a batch and pop in his favorite movie. Make it a movie night he won't soon forget.

1 Pour the vegetable oil into a large, heavy skillet, preferably cast iron, and heat to 350 degrees.

2 Mix the cornmeal and flour together in a medium bowl. Season to taste with salt and pepper.

3 In a separate bowl, combine the okra and buttermilk. Let marinate for 15 minutes. Drain okra and dredge in the cornmeal mixture to coat well.

4 In batches, carefully add the okra to the hot oil and cook until golden brown. Remove from the oil and drain on a paper towel-lined platter. Season with salt and pepper while hot and serve immediately.

MAKES 6 TO 8 SERVINGS

INGREDIENTS

2 cups vegetable oil

1/2 cup cornmeal

1/2 cup flour

Salt and freshly ground black pepper

5 cups
(about 2-1/2 pounds)
fresh okra,
sliced 1/2 inch thick

1 cup buttermilk

It's Not His Mama's... But It Comes Close

Simply *Sweet* Cornbread

INGREDIENTS

1 cup all-purpose flour

1 cup yellow cornmeal

2/3 cup sugar

1 teaspoon salt

1 tablespoon baking powder

2 eggs

1 cup milk

1/3 cup vegetable oil

3 tablespoons
unsalted butter, melted

*S*weet, crumbly cornbread that is so good it will melt in your mouth.

1 Preheat oven to 400 degrees. Spray or lightly grease a 9-inch cast iron skillet or cake pan.

2 Combine flour, cornmeal, sugar, salt, and baking powder in a large bowl.

3 In a separate bowl, combine the eggs, milk, vegetable oil, and butter until well mixed. Slowly stir the egg mixture into the cornmeal mixture and mix just until combined. Pour batter into prepared skillet.

4 Bake for 20 to 25 minutes, or until a toothpick inserted into the center of the cornbread comes out clean.

MAKES 12 SERVINGS

Red Velvet Cake

*S*lip on that red dress Johnny Gill sang about and serve him up a slice of cake. My, My, My!

CAKE

1 Preheat oven to 350 degrees. Grease and flour three 8-inch cake pans and set aside.

2 Cream the sugar and butter together in a large mixing bowl, using an electric mixer on high speed. Beat until light and fluffy, about 3 minutes. Add the eggs, one at a time, and mix well after each addition. In a separate bowl, mix the cocoa powder and food color together and add to the sugar mixture. Mix well.

3 Sift the flour and salt together in a large bowl. Slowly add the flour mixture to the sugar mixture alternately with the buttermilk. Blend in the vanilla. Combine baking soda and vinegar in a small bowl and add to mixture. Pour batter into the prepared pans.

4 Bake until the top springs back when pressed lightly in the center, about 20 to 25 minutes. Remove from heat and cool completely on a wire rack before frosting.

FROSTING

1 Using an electric mixer on high speed, blend cream cheese and butter together in a large mixing bowl until smooth. Lower the mixer speed and add the marshmallow crème, extracts, and confectioners' sugar, and blend just until combined.

2 Spread evenly between layers and on top and sides of cooled cake. Garnish with crushed pecans around the side of the cake.

MAKES 16 TO 20 SERVINGS

INGREDIENTS

CAKE

2 cups granulated sugar

2 sticks unsalted butter, room temperature

2 large eggs, room temperature

1 tablespoon Dutch-processed cocoa powder

2 tablespoons red food color

2-1/2 cups cake flour

1 teaspoon salt

1 cup buttermilk, room temperature

1 teaspoon vanilla extract

1/2 teaspoon baking soda

1 tablespoon vinegar

FROSTING

1 (8-ounce) package cream cheese, room temperature

8 tablespoons unsalted butter, room temperature

1 cup marshmallow crème (recommended: Fluff)

1/4 teaspoon vanilla extract

1/4 teaspoon almond extract

1 (1-pound) box confectioners' sugar

1 cup pecans, crushed (optional)

It's Not His Mama's... But It Comes Close

The Get 'Em Girl's Grown 'N Sexy Checklist

CHECK LIST

☐ **SAFETY FIRST!**
Ladies, we know this is a cookbook, and condoms and Cornish hens don't mix—but we're saying it anyway!

☐ **GOOD SHEETS!**
What makes a quality sheet, you ask? Hmm, let's see— the material, preferably 100% cotton; the thread count, ideally, two hundred and up; and the hand, basically how it feels against your skin. If you are a tee shirt and panties kind of girl or if your budget is tight, a good set of jersey sheets will do just fine! Oh, and have an extra pillow, just in case you don't want to share the four you have on your bed!

☐ **CANDLES!**
Pillar, tea light, soy, or gel…the choices and fragrances are endless.

☐ **AN EXTRA TOOTHBRUSH!**
Morning breath is not cute, so be considerate and hook him up!

Grown 'N Sexy

So Seductive MENU

Pairs Well With: ACACIA CARNEROS CHARDONNAY

OYSTER BISQUE

SALMON WITH BROWN SUGAR GLAZE

SAUTÉED GARLIC ASPARAGUS

KISS O' HONEY POTATOES

HAZELNUT CHOCOLATE-DIPPED STRAWBERRIES

Simple 'N Sexy MENU

Pairs Well With: EXCELSIOR CABERNET SAUVIGNON

BALSAMIC GLAZED ROAST CHICKEN

EASY LIKE...SLOW ROASTED BEEF WITH POTATOES AND GRAVY

BROCCOLI WITH GARLIC AND PARMESAN

SAVORY RICE

CRUSTY FRENCH BAGUETTE (STORE BOUGHT)

EASY STRAWBERRY SHORTCAKE

Sensual Substitutes

FETTUCCINI ALFREDO WITH SHRIMP

HOMEMADE VANILLA ICE CREAM WITH BROWN SUGAR PEACHES

> *If the meal is good I'm always appreciative,*
> *if the meal is bad... it's the thought that counts.*
> *Just knowing that she wants to please me is what matters.*
>
> -JERRY GREEN *New York, NY*

*a*fter five dates, two dozen roses, and six walks in the park, you've decided to invite him over for a nice dinner at your place. You've got the wine on ice, candles lit, Floetry playing, and the Victoria Secret's tucked away in your bottom drawer waiting for the right moment to make its appearance - this is not a Chinese food night!

Call all of your girls and let them know you are not to be disturbed and run through your checklist to make sure you have everything needed to make this a memorable, delicious, and safe evening.

Now that you have covered all of the basics it's time to prepare the meal. You try to remember all of the foods that he mentioned he likes. Whether he's allergic to seafood or if it's his favorite dish; if he is a meat and potatoes guy or a vegetarian— and you plan accordingly.

The recipes included in this section consist of foods that are not only delicious, but are known for their amorous effect on the body, which will make it an evening the both of you will never forget.

Oyster Bisque

a hearty and thick soup. Serve in a crusty bread bowl, and turn this simple soup into an elegant start to a great dinner.

1 In a medium pot over low heat, combine the oysters and the oyster liqueur with a pinch of salt and white pepper, and cover. Cook and stir occasionally until the edges of oysters begin to curl, about 5 minutes.

2 Remove the oysters from the pot with a slotted spoon and set aside. Add the celery, shallots, and water. Cook and stir until tender. Transfer the celery mixture, with the liquid, to a bowl and stir in the half-and-half. Set aside.

3 Melt the butter over low heat and whisk in the flour to make a roux. Add the celery mixture to the roux and stir until it begins to thicken.

4 Place oysters on a cutting board and chop into bite-size pieces; stir into the thickened oyster stock and season to taste with hot pepper sauce. Garnish with chopped parsley and serve immediately.

MAKES 4 SERVINGS

APHRODISIAC ALERT!

Oysters! Ask Casanova – This is the ultimate passion food!

INGREDIENTS

2 (12-ounce) containers shucked oysters in their own liqueur

Kosher salt

Ground white pepper

1/4 cup finely chopped celery

3 tablespoons minced shallots

1/4 cup water

1 quart half-and-half

3 tablespoons butter

1-1/2 teaspoons all-purpose flour

Hot pepper sauce

Chopped fresh parsley, for garnish

Salmon With
Brown Sugar Glaze

INGREDIENTS

2 tablespoons
light brown sugar

2 teaspoons honey

2 tablespoons butter

3 tablespoons
Dijon-style mustard

4-1/2 teaspoons soy sauce

4-1/2 teaspoons olive oil

2 teaspoons
dried ground ginger

4 salmon fillets
(about 6-ounces each)

Vegetable oil

Salt and freshly ground
black pepper

This seductive and sexy salmon dish is glazed with brown sugar and a hint of Dijon-style mustard.

1 In a small saucepan over medium-high heat, melt the brown sugar, honey, and butter. Remove from heat and whisk in the mustard, soy sauce, olive oil, and ground ginger. Set aside.

2 Preheat a grill pan over medium heat. Brush salmon with vegetable oil and season to taste with salt and pepper.

3 Place the salmon skin-side down on the grill. Coat the flesh of the salmon fillets with the brown sugar mixture. Grill for 6 to 8 minutes to medium doneness, turning once after 5 to 6 minutes. Remove from pan and serve immediately.
MAKES 2 TO 4 SERVINGS

APHRODISIAC ALERT!

GINGER! Egyptians used it to ward off impotence —you can use it to kick up your salmon (smile).

Sauteed *Garlic* *Asparagus*

*T*wo powerful passion foods combined makes for an explosive and delicious meal. Tread lightly.

1 Melt butter in a large skillet over medium-high heat. Once the butter is melted, add the garlic, asparagus spears, salt, and pepper.

2 Stirring occasionally, cover and cook until asparagus is tender, about 10 minutes.

MAKES 4 SERVINGS

APHRODISIAC ALERT!

ASPARAGUS! Most erotic member of the vegetable family — particularly stimulating for men!

GARLIC! Promotes virility, strength, and bad breath —make sure you have mints on hand!

INGREDIENTS

3 tablespoons butter

1 bunch (about 1/2-pound) fresh asparagus, tough ends removed

2 cloves garlic, chopped

1/4 teaspoon Kosher salt

1/4 teaspoon freshly ground black pepper

Kiss O' Honey
Potatoes

INGREDIENTS

1-pound small unpeeled
red potatoes,
scrubbed and halved

2 tablespoons
finely chopped
sweet Vidalia onion

1/4 teaspoon salt

1/4 teaspoon
ground black pepper

3 tablespoons butter, melted

2 tablespoons honey

I teaspoon dry mustard

The slight sweetness of these potatoes will complement any meal you prepare.

1 Preheat oven to 375 degrees. Lightly coat an 11 x 7-inch baking dish with non-stick cooking spray.

2 Arrange potatoes in a single layer in the prepared dish, top with the onion, and season with salt and pepper.

3 In a small bowl, combine melted butter, honey, and dry mustard. Drizzle over the potatoes and onion; stir to coat the potatoes.

4 Bake until tender and golden brown, about 40 to 45 minutes, stirring halfway through the cooking time, serve immediately.

MAKES 4 SERVINGS

APHRODISIAC ALERT!

HONEY! Sweet, sticky, and perfect for drizzling – So addictive, it should come with an age limit!

Hazelnut Chocolate-Dipped Strawberries

*W*ho doesn't love the taste of chocolate and strawberries? Well, we took this delicious dessert a step further by covering ripe and sweet strawberries in rich hazelnut chocolate spread. For an intoxicatingly sweet twist, inject the strawberries with a shot of hazelnut liqueur, such as Frangelico!

1 In a small bowl, vigorously whisk together the hazelnut chocolate spread and the cream until it reaches the consistency of melted chocolate. Set aside.

2 Carefully spear strawberries with toothpicks. Working quickly, swirl each strawberry gently in the chocolate mixture, about halfway up the fruit. Place the strawberries on a parchment paper-lined platter. Serve immediately or chill in the refrigerator to harden slightly.

MAKES 4 SERVINGS

APHRODISIAC ALERT!

CHOCOLATE!
Said to release the same chemical that the brain releases during sex! So that's why it's so good!

STRAWBERRIES!
Don't they just look sexy? You feel sexier when eating them – we know!

INGREDIENTS

1 pint fresh strawberries, washed and patted dry, stems intact, and thoroughly air-dried

1 cup hazelnut chocolate spread (recommended: Nutella)

1 tablespoon heavy cream

Balsamic Glazed
Roast Chicken

INGREDIENTS

1 (4-1/2-pound)
roasting chicken

2 sprigs fresh rosemary,
about 1 tablespoon chopped

1 clove garlic, chopped

1 teaspoon poultry seasoning

1/2 tablespoon kosher salt

1 teaspoon ground
black pepper

3 tablespoons butter,
melted

1 tablespoon olive oil

3 tablespoons
balsamic vinegar

1/2 teaspoon brown sugar

Chicken seasoned with aromatic fresh rosemary and drizzled with a sweet balsamic glaze adds a wonderful twist on basic roasted chicken. Serve with Savory Rice. (RECIPE PAGE 46)

1 Preheat oven to 375 degrees.

2 Remove the giblets from the chicken and rinse under cold water. Pat dry with paper towels. Rinse the chicken well, inside and out, under cold water. Pat the chicken dry with paper towels, being sure to dry the body cavity as well.

3 In a small bowl, mix together the rosemary, garlic, poultry seasoning, salt, and pepper. Place the chicken on a rack in a roasting pan just large enough to hold the chicken. Place the giblets in the pan.

4 Season the inside of the chicken with half of the herb mixture. Rub the melted butter and olive oil over chicken. Season the outside of the chicken with the remaining herb mixture.

5 Roast, uncovered, basting with the pan juices every 15 minutes, until a meat thermometer inserted in the thickest part of the thigh reads 170 degrees, about 1 hour, 30 minutes. Meanwhile, mix together in a small bowl the balsamic vinegar and the brown sugar. Set aside.

6 Transfer the chicken to a serving platter. Drizzle with the balsamic vinegar mixture. Carve and scatter with remaining rosemary sprigs.

MAKES 4 SERVINGS

Easy Like... Slow *Roasted Beef* And *Potatoes with Gravy*

*S*ucculent oven roasted beef with a delicious gravy seasoned with thyme, onions, and garlic. A great recipe for a Sunday dinner date with the man of your dreams.

1 Preheat oven to 275 degrees.

2 Season the beef on all sides with the seasoned salt, black pepper, and garlic powder. In a large Dutch oven, heat the vegetable oil over medium-high heat. Add the beef and brown on all sides, about 4 minutes per side. Transfer the meat to a plate and set aside.

3 Stir in the onion slices and the thyme sprigs and cook until the onions are tender, about 3 minutes. Return the meat to the pot, fat side up. Add the beef broth to the pot and place in the oven, uncovered.

4 Roast for 1 hour and remove from the oven. Add the potatoes to the pot; cover and return to the oven. Continue roasting until the beef is tender and the internal temperature registers 130 to 135 degrees, about 30 to 40 minutes.

5 Remove from the oven. Using a slotted spoon, transfer the roast and the potatoes to a serving platter and let rest for 15 minutes before carving. Discard the onions and thyme sprigs.

6 In a small bowl, mix the cornstarch and water until dissolved. Place the Dutch oven over medium-high heat and gradually stir the cornstarch mixture into remaining liquid and bring to a boil.

7 Reduce heat and continue to cook, stirring constantly until thickened, about 3 minutes. Season to taste with seasoned salt and black pepper. Remove from heat and transfer to a gravy boat or decorative bowl.

8 Carve the roast and arrange the slices on a large plate. Arrange the potatoes around the roast and drizzle gravy over each portion. Serve hot.

MAKES 6 TO 8 SERVINGS

INGREDIENTS

1 (3-1/2-pound) bottom round rump roast

1 teaspoon seasoned salt, plus more to taste

1/2 teaspoon freshly ground black pepper, plus more to taste

1/4 teaspoon garlic powder

3 tablespoons vegetable oil

1 medium onion, sliced

3 sprigs fresh thyme

3 cups low-sodium beef broth

2 tablespoons cornstarch

1/4 cup water

8 small unpeeled red potatoes, scrubbed

Broccoli With
Garlic And *Parmesan*

INGREDIENTS

1/4 cup water

2 cups (about 1-pound)
broccoli florets

2 tablespoons
extra virgin olive oil

1 tablespoon butter

2 cloves garlic,
finely chopped

1/4 teaspoon kosher salt

1/4 teaspoon
ground white pepper

1/4 pound Parmesan cheese

1 In a large skillet over medium-high heat, bring 1/4 cup of lightly salted water to a boil. Add the broccoli to the skillet, cover and simmer for 3 minutes. Drain and remove the broccoli from the pan.

2 Add the olive oil, butter, and garlic to the skillet; cook and stir for 3 minutes over medium heat. Add the broccoli, stirring to coat with the oil. Season with salt and pepper.

3 Transfer broccoli to a serving dish and garnish with shaved Parmesan cheese.

MAKES 2 TO 4 SERVINGS

INGREDIENTS

1 cup uncooked
long-grain rice

2 cups low-sodium
beef broth

4 tablespoons butter

1/2 teaspoon salt

1/2 teaspoon ground
white pepper

Savory Rice

1 In a medium saucepan, bring the beef broth to a rapid boil over high heat. Add the rice, butter, salt and pepper. Reduce heat to low and cover tightly. *2* Simmer until the liquid is absorbed and the rice is tender, about 25 to 30 minutes. Remove from heat and let stand, covered, for 5 minutes. Fluff the rice with a fork and serve hot. **MAKES 2 TO 4 SERVINGS**

Easy *Strawberry Shortcake*

*W*hipped topping and strawberries—what more do you need to complete a Grown 'N Sexy evening?

1 Place one slice of cake on each plate. Cover cake slices with strawberries and their juice, and whipped topping. Top with another slice of cake and cover with more strawberries and whipped topping.

2 Garnish each serving with one whole strawberry and serve immediately.

MAKES 4 SERVINGS

INGREDIENTS

1 (12-ounce) ready-made pound cake, cut into 8 slices

1 (16-ounce) container frozen and sweetened sliced strawberries, thawed

1 (8-ounce) container frozen whipped topping, thawed (recommended: Cool Whip)

4 whole strawberries, for garnish

Fettuccine Alfredo
With *Shrimp*

INGREDIENTS

1/2 box (8 ounces)
fettuccine pasta

1/2 cup butter

15 medium shrimp,
peeled and deveined

1/8 teaspoon garlic powder

1/2 teaspoon salt

1/4 teaspoon
freshly ground
black pepper

1-1/2 cups heavy cream

1 cup fresh
Parmesan cheese, grated

This dish is so simple; you will wonder how it could possibly taste so good!

1 Bring a large pot of lightly salted water to a boil. Stir in the fettuccine and cook according to package directions for al dente. Drain and set aside.

2 Meanwhile, in a large saucepan over medium heat, melt the butter. Add the shrimp to the melted butter and season with garlic powder, salt and pepper; cook and stir until shrimp turn pink throughout, about 1 to 2 minutes.

3 Lower heat and stir in cream. Add the Parmesan into the cream mixture and stir constantly until the cheese is melted and the sauce thickens.

4 Transfer pasta to a serving dish, and cover with the shrimp alfredo sauce. Toss to thoroughly coat pasta with the sauce and top with more grated Parmesan cheese. Serve immediately.

MAKES 4 SERVINGS

Homemade *Vanilla Ice Cream*
With *Brown Sugar Peaches*

Ok, I know you are probably looking at the book like, "Are they crazy?" Relax and walk with us. How impressive would it be to have someone actually make you a batch of ice cream — in 2007? I know, very impressive. So, get out the ice cream machine that you received as a housewarming gift and let's show this man that this is not a game!

HOMEMADE VANILLA ICE CREAM

1 Pour the heavy whipping cream into a large, heavy-bottom saucepan. Split open the vanilla bean and scrape out the seeds into the cream. Add the entire vanilla bean to the cream. Over medium heat, bring almost to a boil, then remove from the heat and let the flavors infuse for 30 minutes.

2 Meanwhile, in a large bowl, whisk together the egg yolks and sugar until pale and the mixture leaves a trail when the whisk is lifted. Remove the vanilla bean from the cream mixture and slowly add the cream to the egg mixture, stirring constantly with a wooden spoon.

3 Pour the cream and egg mixture through a mesh strainer into a clean, large, heavy-bottom sauce pan or a double boiler. Cook over low heat for 10 to 15 minutes, stirring constantly until the mixture thickens enough to coat the back of the spoon. Do not let the mixture boil.

4 Remove the custard from the heat and let cool for at least 1 hour, stirring every 15 minutes to prevent a skin from forming.

5 Using an ice-cream machine, churn the cold custard in the machine following the manufacturer's instructions. Once set, spoon ice cream into a freezer-proof container and place in the freezer.

MAKES 4 TO 6 SERVINGS

BROWN SUGAR PEACHES CONTINUED ON NEXT PAGE

INGREDIENTS

**HOME MADE
ICE CREAM**

2-1/2 cups
heavy whipping cream

1 vanilla bean

4 large egg yolks

1/2 cup
confectioners' sugar

Homemade *Vanilla Ice Cream*
With *Brown Sugar Peaches*

INGREDIENTS

**BROWN SUGAR
PEACHES**

1/4 cup unsalted butter

6 tablespoons
light brown sugar, packed

3/4 teaspoon
ground cinnamon

2 cups frozen peaches,
thawed

2 teaspoons vanilla extract

BROWN SUGAR PEACHES

1 In a large, heavy bottom skillet over medium heat, melt the butter. Add the brown sugar and cinnamon and cook, stirring often, until sugar begins to dissolve.

2 Add peaches; cook and stir until peaches are tender and sauce begins to thicken, about 5 minutes.

3 Remove skillet from heat and stir in the vanilla extract. Spoon peaches and sauce over ice cream.

MAKES 4 TO 6 SERVINGS

The *Morning After*

The Cops Came Knockin'! MENU

BUTTERMILK WAFFLES WITH CRISP BACON

VEGGIE AND CHEESE OMELET

Let's Do It Again! MENU

CINNAMON FRENCH TOAST

SCRAMBLED CHEESE EGGS

HOME-FRIED POTATOES

SAGE SAUSAGE

Good Morning, Sunshine! MENU

SALMON CAKES

TOAST WITH APPLE BUTTER SPREAD

CHEDDAR CHEESE GRITS

The Morning After

*T*he dinner was a success; now it's time to send him on his way completely turned out. Ok, we are assuming that he stayed the night. If you set it off the way you should have, he is probably curled up in the fetal position, on your lavender-scented sheets right now.

So here it is, the morning after, and you want to fix him breakfast. Now before you whip out the eggs and bacon, ask yourself… what type of breakfast did his performance warrant? Was it a cornflakes and milk type of performance? Was it a protein shake and yogurt type of performance? If you're lucky it was none of those things and we can skip straight to the omelet, waffles, and homemade muffin type of performance. All jokes aside, if he was privileged enough to get past the bedroom doors and stay the night, make sure you send him off in pure Get 'Em Girl fashion, with wonderful memories and a full stomach.

Buttermilk Waffles
And Crisp Bacon

You are sure to impress him with this breakfast dish. Add some freshly squeezed orange juice to the menu, and don't be surprised if he sticks around for lunch.

1 Preheat waffle iron and lightly spray with nonstick cooking spray.

2 In a large bowl, sift together the flour, baking powder, baking soda, salt, and sugar.

3 In a separate bowl whisk the egg, buttermilk, and melted butter until combined.

4 Add the buttermilk mixture to the flour mixture and stir until smooth.

5 Pour batter into hot waffle iron, being careful not to overfill the iron and cook until golden brown and lightly crisp. Remove and top with a pat of butter if desired, and warm maple syrup.

6 Prepare bacon according to the package instructions Drain the excess grease on a paper towel-lined platter before serving.

MAKES 2 SERVINGS

INGREDIENTS

1 cup all-purpose flour

1 teaspoon baking powder

1/4 teaspoon baking soda

1/4 teaspoon salt

1/4 teaspoon sugar

1 large egg

1 cup buttermilk

4 tablespoons unsalted butter, melted

6 thick slices of bacon (pork or turkey)

Freshly Squeezed Orange Juice

1 Repeatedly roll oranges against hard surface to soften. Cut into halves and remove seeds. With a paring knife, carefully cut around the edge of the orange half, slightly separating the fruit and peel. *2* Grip orange tightly and squeeze continuously directly into a glass or pitcher until liquid is no longer produced. For less pulp, pour juice through a fine strainer before serving. **MAKES 2 (4-OUNCE) SERVINGS**

INGREDIENTS
4 Navel oranges

Veggie
And *Cheese Omelet*

INGREDIENTS

3 large eggs

2 tablespoons heavy cream

1/8 teaspoon salt

1/8 teaspoon
ground white pepper

1 tablespoon
unsalted butter, melted

1 tablespoon diced
green bell pepper

1 tablespoon diced
red bell pepper

1 tablespoon diced onion

4 tablespoons grated
cheddar cheese

*t*he perfect protein food to get him up and going – again and again!

1 In a small bowl, whisk the eggs, heavy cream, salt, and white pepper until frothy. Heat an omelet pan over medium heat; add the butter to the pan, swirling to coat. Add the peppers and onions; cook and stir until tender, about 2 minutes.

2 Pour the egg mixture into the pan. Using a rubber spatula, pull the cooked egg away from the pan and allow the raw egg to run onto the hot part of the pan. When almost set, sprinkle with 3 tablespoons of the cheddar cheese.

3 Cook about 10 seconds longer and use the rubber spatula to fold the omelet in half. Top with the remaining tablespoon of cheese and carefully slide the omelet out of the pan and onto a plate.

MAKES 1 SERVING

Cinnamon French Toast

*t*hick and delicious, this is what French toast is supposed to taste like.

1 Bring the maple syrup, 1 tablespoon butter, and 1 teaspoon cinnamon to a boil in a small saucepan over medium heat. Boil for 2 minutes and remove from heat.

2 Whisk the eggs, heavy cream, vanilla, nutmeg, 3 tablespoons of the syrup mixture, and the remaining 1 teaspoon cinnamon in a bowl. Place bread slices in a large baking dish. Pour egg mixture over the bread, turning to coat. Pierce bread with a fork. Let stand for 3 minutes.

3 Melt 2 tablespoons of butter in a heavy, large skillet over medium heat. Add bread and cook until the edges are slightly crisp and golden brown, about 2 to 3 minutes. Add the remaining 2 tablespoons of butter to skillet. Turn over bread and cook until brown, about 2 to 3 minutes. Transfer to a plate and serve with the remaining syrup.

MAKES 2 SERVINGS

INGREDIENTS

1/2 cup pure maple syrup

4 tablespoons unsalted butter

2 teaspoons ground cinnamon

3 large eggs

1 cup heavy whipping cream

1/2 teaspoon vanilla extract

1/8 teaspoon nutmeg

4 (1-inch thick) brioche bread slices

Scrambled
Cheese Eggs

INGREDIENTS

3 tablespoons butter

5 large eggs

1/2 teaspoon salt

1/2 teaspoon
freshly ground
white pepper

2 tablespoons water

1/2 cup grated
cheddar cheese

*t*hese moist and cheesy eggs will melt in his mouth.

1 Melt the butter in a large, heavy skillet over medium heat. In a small bowl, briskly whisk together the eggs, salt, pepper and 2 tablespoons water. Pour the egg mixture into the skillet.

2 Reduce heat to low, and gently stir egg mixture. Stir in cheddar cheese and continue stirring until desired texture is achieved. Eggs will thicken and dry out very quickly toward the end, so be careful to remove from heat promptly if you like your eggs soft and moist.

MAKES 2 SERVINGS

Home-Fried Potatoes

*C*hunky potatoes and caramelized onions, seasoned to perfection.

HOME-FRIED POTATOES

1 Heat the olive oil and butter in a large skillet over medium heat. Add onions and cook until caramelized, about 10 to 15 minutes. Add potatoes, water, and all seasonings. Cover with lid.

2 Cook for 8 to 10 minutes and flip once with a spatula to brown the other side. Be sure to turn only once to prevent breaking up the potatoes. Continue to cook until the potatoes are fork-tender, about 5 minutes. Serve immediately.

SAGE SAUSAGE

Prepare according to package instructions. Slice into four 1-inch pieces and drain excess grease on a paper towel-lined platter, before serving.

MAKES 2 TO 4 SERVINGS

INGREDIENTS

HOME-FRIED POTATOES

2 tablespoons olive oil

2 tablespoons butter

1 medium onion, chopped

4 large russet potatoes, peeled and sliced 1/4 inch thick

1/2 teaspoon water

1 teaspoon seasoned salt

1/8 teaspoon garlic powder

1/2 teaspoon black pepper

SAGE SAUSAGE

1-1/2 pound package sweet sage sausage

Salmon Cakes

INGREDIENTS

1/2 cup vegetable oil

1/4 cup all-purpose flour

1/4 cup bread crumbs

1 (14.75-ounce) can pink salmon, flaked and de-boned

1 egg, beaten

2 tablespoons chopped yellow onion

1/2 teaspoon seasoned salt

1/4 teaspoon ground black pepper

*t*hese delicious pan-fried salmon cakes are easy to prepare and even easier to devour, especially with a hot serving of Cheese Grits.
(CHEESE GRITS RECIPE ON PAGE 60)

1 Heat the vegetable oil in a medium heavy skillet over medium heat. Mix the flour and bread crumbs together in a medium bowl. In a separate bowl, combine the salmon, egg, onion, seasoned salt, black pepper and 1/4 cup of the flour mixture. Mix well and form into patties. Dust each cake with remaining flour mixture.

2 Fry until golden brown, about 2 to 3 minutes on each side. Drain on a paper towel-lined platter and serve immediately.
MAKES 2 TO 4 SERVINGS

Toast With Apple Butter Spread

Show him your creative skills by whipping up this smooth and delightful spread. Who knew toast could taste so good? Unused apple butter spread can be stored in the refrigerator for up to two weeks.

1 Heat a large grill pan over medium-high heat and toast the brioche slices, turning once.

2 Spread 1/2 teaspoon of butter on each side and set aside.

3 For the apple butter spread: whip the cream cheese and apple butter together in a medium bowl.

4 Spread on toast and serve immediately.

MAKES 2 TO 4 SERVINGS

INGREDIENTS

4 slices brioche
(about 1-inch thick)

2 teaspoons butter,
room temperature

1 (8-ounce) package
cream cheese,
room temperature

1 cup apple butter

Cheddar Cheese Grits

INGREDIENTS

2 cups water

1-1/4 cups milk

1 teaspoon salt,
plus more to taste

1 cup quick-cooking grits
(not instant)

8 tablespoons butter

1/2 cup cheddar cheese,
shredded

Freshly ground
black pepper

1 In a small pot, bring water, milk and salt to a boil. Slowly stir in grits. Stir continuously until grits are mixed well. Let the pot return to a boil, cover with a tightly fitting lid and reduce the temperature to low.

2 Simmer for approximately 30 minutes, stirring occasionally. Add more water if necessary. Once grits have a smooth and creamy consistency, remove from heat.

3 Stir in 4 tablespoons of butter and the cheddar cheese. Stir until the cheese is melted and incorporated thoroughly. Season to taste, with additional salt and pepper. Serve hot with butter.

MAKES 4 SERVINGS

A *Trip* For *Two*

Yo Quiero Papi MENU

BROILED CHICKEN

CREAMED SPINACH

SPANISH YELLOW RICE

FRIED SWEET PLANTAINS

TRES LECHES (THREE MILKS) CAKE

GET 'EM GIRL SANGRIA

Island Hoppin' MENU

COCONUT SHRIMP

STEAMED RED SNAPPER

CURRIED CHICKEN

GOONGO PEAS AND RICE

STEAMED CALLALOO

COCONUT CREAM PARFAIT

Asian MENU

SHRIMP EGG ROLLS

HOISIN-GLAZED PORK CHOPS

VEGETABLE FRIED RICE

FLIRTY FORTUNE COOKIES

MINT ICED GREEN TEA

> I knew my college sweetheart had the potential to be my wife after she cooked for me on our second date. Girls I knew were using ketchup and lemon juice to season their chicken, but my baby had her own special barbecue marinade.
>
> -PHOENIX EVANS *Greenville, NC*

*i*t is twenty degrees outside on a snowy evening and the last thing you want to do is go out for dinner and a movie in this weather. How about inviting him over for some fun, food, and fantasies? Just imagine: snow and sleet outside and Caribbean grooves inside.

First and foremost, you have to set the stage for the evening. If it is a Caribbean theme you're going for, pick up a Bob Marley greatest hits CD to set the mood for the evening. Stop at your local party store and pick up some tropical themed props, (i.e. raffia table skirts, coconut cups, or island-inspired tableware and place settings).

For a little Latin flair, pop in some Novalima or Carlos Santana to set the mood, whip up a pitcher of delicious Sangria with glasses to match, and pickup some inexpensive and practical serving pieces that will set the tone and create the atmosphere you want to evoke.

To create an Asian-inspired evening, how about purchasing some bamboo mats, chopsticks, and theme-centered place settings for two? For added effect, pick up a sexy kimono to wear for the evening.

Just the fact that you were inventive and thoughtful enough to create this type of experience for him will leave a lasting impression, and once he tastes the delicious meal you've cooked, he'll be wondering which exotic "trip" you two are going on next. Hey, just think… he might plan something special on his own… Well, you never know!

RECIPE ON PAGE
19

Simple *Southern* *Fried Chicken*

RECIPE ON PAGE

III

Homemade
Tortilla Chips

Broiled Chicken

This is a simple and easy dish that is full of Latin flavor. Served with yellow rice, this is sure to be a winner

1 Rinse and clean chicken, pat dry, and place in a resealable plastic bag. Mix the olive oil, vinegar, salt, pepper, oregano, and garlic in a bowl. Pour over the chicken. Close bag, releasing any air, and rub seasoning thoroughly into chicken parts. Refrigerate for 6 hours or preferably overnight.

2 When ready to cook, preheat broiler.

3 Remove chicken from bag and discard the remaining marinade. Broil chicken in a pan, turning once and basting frequently with pan juices until juices run clear and no pink shows, about 30 minutes. Serve immediately.

MAKES 4 SERVINGS

INGREDIENTS

1 (3-pound) chicken, cut into 8 pieces

1/2 cup olive oil

1-1/2 tablespoons vinegar

1 teaspoon salt

1 teaspoon freshly ground black pepper

1 teaspoon dried oregano

2 cloves garlic, crushed

Spanish Yellow Rice

1 Heat the olive oil in a medium saucepan over medium heat. Add the onion and green pepper; cook and stir until onion is translucent. Stir in the tomatoes, Sazon packet, salt, and pepper. Continue to cook for 1 minute. *2* Add the chicken stock and bring to a boil. Stir in rice and bring to a second boil. *3* Cover with a tightly fitting lid and reduce heat to low. Simmer until broth is absorbed and rice is tender, about 20 to 25 minutes.

MAKES 4 SERVINGS

INGREDIENTS

2 tablespoons extra virgin olive oil

1/2 cup chopped Spanish onion

1/4 cup chopped green bell pepper

1/2 can (4-ounces) diced tomatoes, drained

2 cups low-sodium chicken broth

1 packet Sazon with annatto

1/2 teaspoon salt

1/4 teaspoon ground black pepper

1 cup long grain or basmati rice

Creamed Spinach

INGREDIENTS

2 (10-ounce) packages frozen chopped spinach, thawed

1/4 teaspoon salt

2 tablespoons butter

1 tablespoon all-purpose flour

3/4 cup milk

1/4 teaspoon ground black pepper

1/8 teaspoon freshly grated nutmeg

1/4 cup grated Parmesan (optional)

*f*ast and easy to prepare, sautéed frozen spinach is added to a roux-thickened mixture of milk, butter, and flour.

1 Place the spinach in a colander over a medium bowl. Squeeze until all the liquid is out of spinach, reserve 1/4 cup of spinach liquid and set aside.

2 In a medium saucepan over medium heat, combine the spinach, 1/4 cup spinach liquid, and salt. Cook and stir for 2 minutes, drain and set aside.

3 Melt the butter in a separate medium saucepan over medium-low heat. Add the flour to the saucepan and whisk until smooth. Slowly add milk and whisk briskly until mixture starts to thicken.

4 Add spinach, black pepper, nutmeg, and Parmesan. Stir to combine and serve immediately.

MAKES 4 SERVINGS

INGREDIENTS

3 very ripe yellow plantains

1/4 cup vegetable oil

Fried Sweet *Plantains (maduros)*

1 Peel the plantains and cut into diagonal slices, about 1/2 inch thick and 3 inches long. *2* Heat the vegetable oil in a small skillet over medium-low heat. Fry in hot oil until slightly browned and tender, about 3 minutes. Carefully flip plantains with a spatula and cook until slightly browned.

MAKES 2 TO 4 SERVINGS

Tres Leches (Three Milks) Cake

Chill to almost frozen – this ice cream cake-like dessert will cool down all the heat created during dinner... that is, if you're trying to cool it down!

1 Prepare the yellow cake according to the package directions for a 9 x 13-inch cake pan. Let cool completely in the cake pan.

2 Meanwhile, in a large bowl, combine the heavy cream with the evaporated and condensed milks. Mix well and set aside.

3 Poke holes all over cake with a fork and pour the milk mixture over cake. Cover with plastic wrap and refrigerate for 4 hours.

4 Remove from the refrigerator and cover with whipped topping. Sprinkle with coconut and serve immediately.

MAKES 6 TO 8 SERVINGS

INGREDIENTS

1 (18.25-ounce) package yellow cake mix with pudding added

1 pint heavy cream

1 (12-ounce) can evaporated milk

1 (14-ounce) can sweetened condensed milk

1 (8-ounce) container frozen whipped topping, thawed

1/4 cup sweetened flaked coconut (optional)

Get 'Em Girl
Sangria

INGREDIENTS

1 (750 ml) bottle of sweet white wine, chilled
(recommended: Vision Cellars Riesling 2005)

1/2 cup peach schnapps
(recommended: DeKuyper's)

2 cups frozen sliced peaches

1 orange, cut into wedges

1 Granny Smith apple, cut into wedges

1/4 cup granulated sugar

2 cups ginger ale

*a*dd a little sizzle to your evening with our delicious and potent drink. Sip slowly and enjoy!

1 Pour the wine and peach schnapps into a large pitcher. Stir in the peaches, orange and apple wedges. Add the sugar to the pitcher and stir to dissolve.

2 Chill the mixture in the refrigerator for 1 hour. Add ginger ale just before serving.

MAKES 6 TO 8 SERVINGS

Coconut Shrimp

Serve as a main dish or appetizer with the delicious Honey-Orange Dipping Sauce.

1 Combine the coconut and bread crumbs in a large bowl. Season to taste with salt and pepper. Divide the flour and eggs into 2 separate bowls.

2 Meanwhile, in a large Dutch oven, heat about 3 inches of vegetable oil to 350 degrees.

3 Dredge the shrimp in the flour, shaking off any excess. Follow by dipping the shrimp in the egg mixture and then coating thoroughly with the coconut mixture.

4 In batches, fry the shrimp until golden brown and cooked through, about 3 to 4 minutes per batch. Remove from the oil and drain on a paper tower-lined platter. Serve immediately.

MAKES 2 TO 4 SERVINGS

INGREDIENTS

1/2 cup sweetened flaked coconut

1/2 cup bread crumbs

Salt and pepper

1/2 cup all-purpose flour

2 large eggs, beaten

Vegetable oil, for frying

12 large shrimp, peeled and deveined

Honey-Orange Dipping Sauce

1 In a small bowl, combine all of the ingredients. *2* Mix well and serve along side coconut shrimp. MAKES ABOUT 8 OUNCES

INGREDIENTS

1/2 cup orange marmalade

1/4 cup Dijon-style mustard

1/4 cup honey

Hot pepper sauce (optional)

Steamed *Red* *Snapper*

INGREDIENTS

4 red snapper fillets,
about 1-pound total

2 teaspoons kosher salt

1-1/2 teaspoons
freshly ground
black pepper

3 tablespoons butter

1 small onion, sliced into
half-moon rings

1 clove garlic, chopped

1 large carrot,
peeled and
sliced diagonally

1 small tomato, chopped

1 small green bell pepper,
seeded and sliced
into 1/2-inch strips

2 sprigs fresh thyme

1/3 cup water

4 cups cabbage,
coarsely chopped

(*i*n our best West Indian accent...) Serve your mon dis authentic island dish and everything will be irie!

1 Season fish with 1 teaspoon salt and 1 teaspoon black pepper.

2 Melt the butter in a large pan over medium heat. Add the fish, onion, garlic, carrot, tomato, bell pepper, thyme and water. Cook, stirring occasionally for 5 minutes.

3 Reduce heat to low, cover and steam for 10 minutes. Add cabbage, season with remaining salt and black pepper, cover and steam for an additional 5 minutes.

4 Transfer to a platter and serve immediately with vegetables on top.
MAKES 2 TO 4 SERVINGS

Curried
Chicken

1 Clean and rinse chicken under cold water. Place in a large bowl and add lemon or lime juice; let sit for 1 minute, rinse well with cold water, and pat dry.

2 In a separate large bowl, combine the onions, potatoes, 2 tablespoons of curry powder, the dried thyme, salt, black pepper, garlic, and sugar. Mix well and let sit for 10 minutes to allow flavors to combine. Add the chicken to the curry mixture and mix well. Cover with plastic wrap and refrigerate for 20 to 30 minutes.

3 Heat the vegetable oil in a large skillet over medium heat. Stir the remaining tablespoon of curry powder and the fresh thyme into the vegetable oil. Carefully add the chicken pieces and brown on all sides, about 10 minutes. Add the remaining ingredients and cover tightly.

4 Reduce heat to low, cover and simmer until chicken is tender and shows no sign of pink, about 25 minutes. Remove from heat and serve immediately.

MAKES 6 TO 8 SERVINGS

INGREDIENTS

1 (2 to 2 1/2-pound) fryer chicken, cut into 8 pieces

1 cup lemon or lime juice

1 large onion, chopped

4 small peeled russet potatoes, cubed

3 tablespoons curry powder

1-1/2 teaspoons dried thyme

2 teaspoons kosher salt

1 teaspoon freshly ground black pepper

2 cloves garlic, chopped

1/2 teaspoon granulated sugar

3 tablespoons vegetable oil

1 stem fresh thyme

1/4 cup chicken stock

Goongo
Peas & Rice

INGREDIENTS

4 cups water

1 (19-ounce) can goongo peas

1 stalk scallion, chopped

1 small onion, chopped

2 sprigs of fresh thyme, chopped

2 teaspoons salt

1 teaspoon freshly ground black pepper

1 clove garlic, chopped

2 cups coconut milk

3 cups uncooked white rice

*P*eas and rice sweetened with coconut milk is a traditional dish throughout the Caribbean. Serve with iron-rich Steamed Callaloo for an authentic Caribbean dining experience.

1 Bring water to boil in a large saucepan. Add the goongo peas, scallion, onion, thyme, salt, pepper, garlic, and coconut milk. Bring to a second boil and cook for 15 minutes.

2 Stir in rice; lower heat, cover, and steam for 25 minutes. Remove from heat and serve immediately.

MAKES 4 TO 6 SERVINGS

INGREDIENTS

1 tablespoon butter

1 medium onion, sliced

2 cups fresh callaloo, washed and chopped

1/4 cup water

1 teaspoon salt

1 teaspoon salt

1/2 teaspoon freshly ground black pepper

Steamed Callaloo

1 Melt the butter in a large saucepan over medium heat. Add the onion and cook until translucent, about 5 minutes. Stir in the callaloo and water. *2* Lower heat, cover saucepan, and simmer until callaloo is tender, about 15 to 20 minutes. Season with salt and pepper. Remove from heat and serve immediately. **MAKES 2 TO 4 SERVINGS**

Coconut Cream Parfait

Smooth custard layered with sweet coconut and crunchy golden graham crackers.

1 In a large bowl, whisk together the pudding mix and milk. Add the vanilla extract and continue to whisk mixture until it thickens. Fold 3/4 cup of coconut and half of the whipped topping into the pudding. Cover with plastic wrap and refrigerate until ready to serve.

2 Sprinkle 1 tablespoon of the graham cracker crumbs into a martini glass or stemmed bowl. Spoon the pudding mixture over the graham crackers. Garnish with more graham crackers and shredded coconut. Serve immediately.

MAKES 2 TO 4 SERVINGS

INGREDIENTS

1 (5-ounce) package instant vanilla pudding mix

1-1/2 cups milk

1/2 teaspoon vanilla extract

1 cup sweetened flaked coconut

1 (8-ounce) container frozen whipped topping, thawed

1/4 cup graham cracker crumbs

Shrimp
Egg Rolls

INGREDIENTS

2 tablespoons peanut
or vegetable oil

4 cups shredded
green cabbage

3 scallion stalks,
thinly sliced

1/2 cup fresh bean sprouts

1 tablespoon soy sauce

1 teaspoon brown sugar

1 cup cooked shrimp,
chopped

1 package egg roll skins

1 egg, beaten

Vegetable oil, for frying

*W*hy order take-out when you can make it yourself?

1 Heat the peanut oil in a large wok or skillet over medium-high heat. Add the cabbage, scallions, and bean sprouts and toss with oil to coat. Raise heat to high and stir-fry until cabbage gets limp, about 3 minutes.

2 Add the soy sauce, light brown sugar, and shrimp. Cook and stir until heated through, about 1 minute. Transfer to a bowl with a slotted spoon and allow to cool completely.

3 Place the egg roll wrappers on a flat work surface, with the tip facing you. Fill the egg roll wrappers with about 1/4 cup of filling per egg roll.

4 To close, fold the tip facing you over the filling towards the center. Lightly brush the side tips of the wrapper with some of the beaten egg, and then fold them into the center, overlapping them if necessary.

5 Brush the tip furthest from you with a little of the beaten egg and fold toward you to seal the egg roll. Repeat with the remaining wrappers and filling. You should have enough filling for 6 to 8 egg rolls.

6 While you are rolling the egg rolls, heat the vegetable oil in a large, heavy-bottom skillet to 350 degrees. Carefully add 2 egg rolls to the vegetable oil and fry, turning frequently with tongs, until golden brown, about 4 to 5 minutes. Repeat with the remaining egg rolls. Serve immediately with Chinese mustard or sweet and sour sauce.

MAKES 6 TO 8 SERVINGS

Hoisin Glazed
Pork Chops

*C*hinese barbeque sauce lightly brushed over thick, juicy chops.

1 Preheat oven to 400 degrees.

2 In a large bowl, whisk together the scallions, hoisin sauce, oyster sauce, mustard, ginger, and honey. Add the pork chops to the bowl and coat with the sauce.

3 Arrange the pork chops in a shallow baking dish. Spoon the remaining sauce over the pork and roast uncovered for 15 to 20 minutes.

4 Turn on the broiler and place the pork chops 5 to 6 inches from heat. Cook until the top is slightly caramelized, about 2 to 5 minutes. Let stand uncovered for 5 minutes. Serve immediately with pan juices.

MAKES 4 SERVINGS

INGREDIENTS

1 bunch scallions, sliced into 2-inch pieces

2 tablespoons plus 1 -1/2 teaspoons hoisin sauce

3 tablespoons oyster sauce

1 tablespoon plus 1 -1/2 teaspoons Dijon-style mustard

1/4 teaspoon fresh ginger, finely grated

2 tablespoons honey

4 center-cut pork chops (about 1-inch thick)

Vegetable
Fried Rice

INGREDIENTS

2 tablespoons vegetable oil

2 cups cooked
long-grain rice, chilled

1 cup frozen
peas and carrots,
thawed

1 teaspoon salt

2 eggs, beaten

1/2 cup fresh bean sprouts

2 tablespoons thinly
sliced scallions

1 Heat a wok or large skillet over high heat. Add the vegetable oil and continue to heat until oil is almost smoking.

2 Add the cooked rice to the wok; cook and stir for 1 minute. Add the peas and carrots and season with salt. Cook and stir for 5 minutes over high heat.

3 Stir the beaten eggs and bean sprouts into the rice mixture and continue to cook until the eggs have set, about 2 minutes. Remove from heat and transfer to a serving bowl. Garnish with the scallions and serve immediately.

MAKES 4 SERVINGS

INGREDIENTS

6 cups water

1/2 cup mint leaves

6 green tea bags

1/4 cup honey

1/4 cup granulated sugar

1 tablespoon
fresh lemon juice

Mint Iced Green Tea

1 In a large saucepan over high heat, bring the water to a boil. Remove from heat and add the mint leaves and tea bags. Cover and let steep for 15 minutes. *2* Strain the tea into a large pitcher and add the honey, sugar, and lemon juice. Refrigerate until chilled. Serve over ice cubes and garnish with additional mint leaves. **MAKES ABOUT 6 (8-OUNCE) SERVINGS**

Flirty *Fortune Cookies*

*i*magine his expression when he reads the sexy and suggestive fortunes you have created just for him.

1 Preheat oven to 300 degrees. Grease 2 baking sheets with non-stick cooking spray and set aside.

2 Write or type flirtatious fortunes on pieces of paper that are 3-1/2 inches long and 1/2 inch wide.

3 In a medium bowl, lightly beat the egg whites, vanilla and almond extracts, and vegetable oil until frothy. In a separate bowl, sift together the flour, cornstarch, salt, and sugar.

4 Stir the water into the flour mixture. Add the flour mixture into the egg white mixture and stir until smooth.

5 Place 1 tablespoon of batter onto one of the prepared baking sheets. Gently tilt the baking sheet back and forth so that the batter forms into a 4-inch circle.

6 Bake until the outer 1/2-inch of the cookie turns golden brown and is easy to remove from the baking sheet with a spatula, about 12 to 14 minutes.

7 Working quickly, remove the cookie with a spatula and flip it over onto a clean, flat work surface or into your hand. Place a fortune in the middle of the cookie and quickly fold in half. Gently pull the edges of the halved cookie downward over the rim of a glass.

8 Place the finished cookie in the cup of a muffin tin so that it keeps its shape. Continue with the rest of the cookies, using the unused baking sheet while the other cools completely.

MAKES 8 TO 9 COOKIES

MAKE IT YOUR OWN

For chocolate-dipped fortune cookies, melt 8-ounces of semi-sweet chocolate and 1 tablespoon of vegetable shortening in a double boiler or a glass bowl over boiling water. Stir continually while melting, making sure not to get any water into the mixture. Dip the bottom of each cookie into the melted chocolate and place on a wax paper-lined cookie sheet. Refrigerate to harden.

INGREDIENTS

2 large egg whites

1/2 teaspoon vanilla extract

1/2 teaspoon almond extract

3 tablespoons vegetable oil

1/2 cup all-purpose flour

1-1/2 teaspoons cornstarch

1/4 teaspoon salt

1/2 cup granulated sugar

1 tablespoon water

Make him say *ahhhhhh...*

*h*ere are some really sweet ideas to make him feel better and help pass the time while he's whining like a big baby and infecting your favorite down blanket with his nasty germs:

BOARD GAMES!
Break out the Scrabble and go easy on him – no triple word scores!

FLOWERS!
Contrary to what you may have heard, men can appreciate a delivery of beautiful flowers just as much as you can.

MAN MOVIES!
Scarface, Reservoir Dogs, Gladiator, The Usual Suspects, and the like...suck it up!

HOT CHOCOLATE
...with whipped cream, shaved chocolate, and marshmallows!

CHILDHOOD CANDIES!
Lemonheads, Boston Baked Beans, Now and Laters, or Mike and Ikes

Soups And Salads
For The Soul

*h*e just called you to let you know he has the cold from hell: his nose is runny, his head is stuffy, and nothing he's taking is working. What he needs is some good old-fashioned homemade soup. How about whipping something up that will not only leave him feeling much better physically, but will having him wondering, "Where have you been all my life?"

Whether it's a pot of cold remedy chicken soup or a light lunch date at his place, the recipes in this section are great as stand-alone dishes, or as quick additions to any meal you are cooking.

Nancy's *Goulash Stew*

$\mathcal{G}$reat advice and beauty tips are not the only two things Nancy in known for. She is also known for burning in the kitchen, and this stew is proof of that!

1 In a large bowl, toss the steak in the seasoned flour and set aside. Meanwhile, melt the butter in a Dutch oven or large pot over medium heat. Add the steak to the pot and brown on all sides.

2 Stir the tomatoes, potatoes, beef broth, and paprika into the pot; bring to boil. Season to taste with salt and pepper.

3 Reduce heat, cover, and simmer for 1/2 hour or until potatoes are tender. Serve in a crusty sourdough bread bowl. Garnish with a dollop of sour cream and dill; serve immediately.

MAKES 6 TO 8 SERVINGS

INGREDIENTS

2 pounds of chuck steak, cubed

1/2 cup flour, seasoned with salt and pepper

4 tablespoons butter

2 (28-ounce) cans whole tomatoes

3 medium peeled russet potatoes, cubed

2 cups beef broth

4 tablespoons paprika

Salt and pepper

1 cup sour cream

Fresh dill, for garnish

Bring-Him-Back
Chicken Soup!

INGREDIENTS

1 (3-pound)
whole chicken, cut up

1 large onion, quartered

1 garlic clove, minced

2 bay leaves

2 chicken bouillon cubes

1 sprig fresh thyme

Salt and pepper to taste

2 carrots, chopped

2 celery stalks, chopped

1-1/2 cups rotini noodles

2 tablespoons
fresh parsley,
chopped

When the nightcaps go from Chardonnay to Nyquil, it's time to kick into Get 'Em Girl mode and bring him back!

1 Wash the chicken under cold water. Place in a large stock pot or Dutch oven with enough water to cover, about 2 quarts. Add the onion, garlic, bay leaves, bouillon cubes, thyme, salt and pepper, and bring to a boil.

2 Reduce heat to low and simmer, partially covered, until the chicken begins to pull away from the bone, about 1 hour. Remove any fat that has risen to the top of the stock with a skimmer or large spoon as it cooks.

3 Remove the chicken from the stock and set aside until cool enough to handle. Remove and discard the bay leaves and onion. Pull the chicken meat off the bones, discarding the bones, skin, and any remaining fat. Chop the meat into bite-size pieces and set aside.

4 Bring stock back to a boil and add the carrots and celery. Reduce heat to medium-low and simmer until the vegetables are tender, about 15 to 20 minutes. Return the meat to the stock and season to taste with additional salt and pepper.

5 Add the rotini noodles and simmer until noodles are cooked through, about 10 to 12 minutes. Remove from the heat and stir in parsley. Serve immediately.

MAKES 4 SERVINGS

INGREDIENTS

1 orange pekoe tea bag

3/4 cup boiling water

1 tablespoon honey

2 ounces brandy

1 slice lemon

Grandma's Hot Toddy

1 Place the tea bag and boiling water in a medium tea cup and let steep for 5 minutes. *2* Remove the tea bag and stir in the honey until completely dissolved. Mix in the brandy and serve with the lemon slice. **MAKES 1 SERVING**

Creamy *Tomato* *Soup*

*W*arm and soothing — goes great with a grilled cheese sandwich.

1 In a Dutch oven over medium heat, cook and stir onions in butter until translucent, about 5 minutes. Remove from heat and stir in the flour, salt, sugar, basil, and white pepper.

2 Add 3/4 cup warm milk and blend well. Gradually add the remaining milk, stirring constantly.

3 Heat the tomatoes in a separate pot, over medium-high heat. Remove from heat and add the baking soda. Let tomatoes stand for 3 minutes and add to the white sauce. Serve immediately.

TIP: For smoother tomato soup, blend with an immersion blender right before serving.
MAKES 4 SERVINGS

INGREDIENTS

1 cup onion, diced

2 tablespoons butter

2 tablespoons all-purpose flour

1 teaspoon salt

1 teaspoon sugar

1/2 teaspoon fresh basil, chopped

1/4 teaspoon ground white pepper

2 cups milk, warm

2 cups canned crushed tomatoes

1/8 teaspoon baking soda

Grilled Cheese... Grown Up!

1 Arrange the cheese on the bottom layer of the bread. Top with the other half of the bread and press firmly to seal. Brush both sides of the sandwich with butter. *2* Lightly butter a heavy skillet. Cook the sandwich over medium-high heat until the cheese is fully melted on the inside and the sandwich is golden brown on both sides, about 4 minutes per side. Slice diagonally and serve immediately. **MAKES 2 SERVINGS**

INGREDIENTS

1 (6x8-inch) piece focaccia, sliced horizontally

4 ounces Havarti cheese, sliced

4 tablespoons butter, room temperature

Dee's *Split Pea Soup*

INGREDIENTS

1-1/2 cups dried split peas

1 (16-ounce) package Kielbasa sausage, chopped into 1/4-inch cubes

1/2 pound ham steak, chopped into 1/4-inch cubes

1 small onion, chopped

Salt and pepper

6 cups cold water, plus more as needed

1 cup chopped carrots

1 small peeled Idaho potato, diced

*W*onderfully warming - comfort food. Grab a blanket, two bowls, and some crusty bread, and make it a movie weekend.

1 Combine the peas, sausage, onion, and ham steak in a large stock pot. Season to taste with salt and pepper, cover with the water, and bring to a boil.

2 Reduce heat to medium-low and simmer for 45 minutes, stirring occasionally, and adding more water if necessary.

3 Add the carrots and potatoes and continue simmering until vegetables are tender, about 15 to 20 minutes. Serve warm with crusty Italian bread.

MAKES 6 SERVINGS

Cajun Gumbo

Add a bit of the Bayou to your menu with this classic Cajun dish.

1 Combine the water and chicken in a large pot over high heat and bring to a boil. Reduce heat to low and simmer until chicken begins to pull away from the bone, about 1 hour. Remove any fat that has risen to the top of the stock with a skimmer or large spoon, as it cooks.

2 Remove the chicken from the stock and set aside until cool enough to handle; reserve the chicken stock. Once cool enough to handle, pull the chicken meat off the bones. Discard the bones, skin, and any remaining fat, and set aside.

3 Heat 2 tablespoons of oil in a heavy skillet over medium heat. Add okra; cook and stir until no longer sticky, about 20 minutes. Set aside.

4 To make the roux, stir flour and 1/4 cup of oil in a large heavy sauce pan or Dutch oven. Cook and stir over medium heat until deep golden brown, about 6 minutes.

5 Stir the onion, celery, green pepper, salt, garlic, black pepper and cayenne pepper into the roux. Cook and stir over medium heat, for 3 minutes.

6 Gradually add 3 cups of the reserved chicken stock, okra, chicken, andouille sausage, tomatoes, and bay leaves, and bring to a boil. Cover partially and reduce heat to low, simmer until thickened, about 1 hour.

7 If desired, serve with 1/4 teaspoon of filé powder to stir into each serving. Serve immediately with white rice.

MAKES 6 SERVINGS

INGREDIENTS

6 cups water

1 (2-pound) chicken, cut up

1/4 cup vegetable oil, plus 2 tablespoons

1 cup sliced okra

1/3 cup all-purpose flour

1/2 cup chopped onion

1/2 cup chopped celery

1/2 cup chopped green pepper

1 teaspoon salt

1 clove garlic, minced

1/2 teaspoon ground black pepper

1/2 teaspoon cayenne pepper

8-ounces andouille sausage, sliced

2 cups canned whole peeled tomatoes

2 bay leaves

1 teaspoon file powder (optional)

Egg Salad
With *Pita Wedges*

INGREDIENTS

4 slices thick-cut bacon

6 large eggs

1/4 cup mayonnaise

1/2 teaspoon salt

1/4 teaspoon
ground black pepper

1/8 teaspoon sweet paprika

2 whole wheat pita pockets,
cut into 4 wedges

*i*nvite him to a nice picnic lunch in the park - or in your bed!

1 Prepare bacon according to package directions. Crumble and set aside.

2 Place the eggs in a medium saucepan with enough cold water to cover and bring to a boil. Cover with a tight-fitting lid and remove from heat. Let the eggs stand in the hot water for 10 to 15 minutes. Remove from hot water and let cool before peeling. Chop and set aside.

3 Mix the chopped eggs, mayonnaise, salt, pepper, and paprika in a large bowl. Mash with a fork. Serve with crumbled bacon sprinkled on top and pita wedges on the side.
MAKES 2 SERVINGS

Bacon And Blue Cheese Wedge Salad

*t*asty enough for a light lunch and hearty enough for a light dinner - store the blue cheese dressing in an airtight jar and refrigerate for up to 3 days.

1 In a medium bowl, combine the mayonnaise, lemon juice, ground black pepper, and hot pepper sauce. Add the blue cheese and stir until well blended. Refrigerate until ready to use.

2 In a large skillet, preferably cast iron, cook the bacon over medium-high heat until golden brown and beginning to crisp.

3 Arrange lettuce on plates and drizzle with dressing. Using a slotted spoon, transfer warm bacon from the skillet onto the salads, dividing equally.

MAKES 6 SERVINGS

INGREDIENTS

1-1/2 cups mayonnaise

4-1/2 teaspoons fresh lemon juice

1-1/2 teaspoons freshly ground black pepper

1 teaspoon hot pepper sauce

1 cup blue cheese, coarsely crumbled

1/2 pound thick-cut bacon, cut into 1-inch pieces

1 large head of iceberg lettuce, cut into 6 wedges

Quick *Side* *Salad*

INGREDIENTS

1 (10-ounce)
bag mixed salad greens,
washed and thoroughly dried

1/2 cup carrots, shredded

1 cup cherry tomatoes, sliced

1/2 cup grated
Parmesan cheese

1 cup creamy
Parmesan salad dressing

1/8 teaspoon freshly
ground black pepper

2 cups croutons

1 In a large salad bowl, combine all ingredients, except croutons, and toss gently. Top with the croutons and serve.

MAKES 4 SERVINGS

Chicken Salad

*a*bsolutely delicious alone or on a crusty Kaiser roll.

1 Wash the chicken under cold water. Place in a large stock pot or Dutch oven with enough water to cover, about 2 quarts. Add the onion, celery stalk, kosher salt, 1/4 teaspoon black pepper and bring to a boil.

2 Reduce the heat to low and simmer until the chicken shows no sign of pink when pierced in the thickest part, about 20 minutes. Remove from heat and let cool in the liquid.

3 Once cool enough to handle, transfer chicken to a platter, remove and discard the skin, bones, and any remaining fat. Strain the chicken stock through a cheesecloth or fine sieve, discarding the onion and celery; reserve and refrigerate the chicken stock in an air-tight jar to use at a later date. Dice the chicken into 3/4-inch pieces and place in a large bowl.

4 Combine the chicken, eggs, diced celery, red onion, pickle relish, seasoned salt, mayonnaise, remaining 1/2 teaspoon black pepper, and crushed red pepper (if using). Mix well. Cover with plastic wrap and refrigerate until ready to serve.

MAKES 6 SERVINGS

INGREDIENTS

1 (3-pound) chicken, cut-up

1 small yellow onion, quartered

1 celery stalk

1/2 teaspoon kosher salt

3/4 teaspoon freshly ground black pepper, divided

4 hard-cooked eggs, chopped (instructions on page 25)

3/4 cup finely diced celery

1/2 cup finely diced red onion

1/2 cup sweet pickle relish

2 teaspoons seasoned salt

1 cup mayonnaise

1/8 teaspoon crushed red pepper flakes (optional)

30 Minutes
Or Less Tips

Although cooking can be pretty time-consuming, it doesn't have to be. Just follow some of our suggestions on speeding up the process and you will have plate to table in no time flat.

MAKE SURE YOUR KITCHEN IS ORGANIZED, with pots near the stove and utensils near your work area.

LEARN TO MULTI-TASK. Read each recipe carefully and look for spaces where you can incorporate 2 or 3 steps. For instance, while you're preheating the oven, begin boiling the water for pasta dishes and defrosting your meat in the microwave.

PREPARE YOUR VEGETABLES AND FRESH HERBS AHEAD OF TIME. When you come in from the grocery store, wash and store all your veggies/herbs in resealable plastic bags, making sure to wrap fresh herbs with a damp paper towel.

SHORTCUTS WORK IN A PINCH. Use bagged salad greens, pre-made pasta sauces, frozen vegetables, grated cheeses, and seasoning blends. Often, they save you time without taking away from the flavor of your dishes.

TRY AND PRE-PLAN YOUR MEALS. You can have your meats thawed, marinated, and ready to cook if you've pre-planned your meal.

30 Minutes Or Less

Mangia, Mangia... in 30! MENU

EFFORTLESS CHICKEN PARMESAN WITH ANGEL HAIR PASTA

CHEDDAR GARLIC BISCUITS

SIMPLE SALAD WITH BALSAMIC VINAIGRETTE

TIRAMISU FOR TWO

If I Had One Dish!

JUMPIN' JUMPIN' JAMBALAYA WITH STEAMED WHITE RICE

JUNIOR'S SHEPHERD'S PIE AND QUICK SIDE SALAD

> Managing your time and creating love through food,
> makes for a healthy and happy relationship.
> -ONI MCDONALD *Baltimore, MD*

*h*e called to let you know how much you have been on his mind, and was wondering if you wanted to have company. He will be leaving work in an hour and wondered if he could stop by for a few.

Normally, you wouldn't even entertain the idea of having company over this late in the week. Your apartment is a wreck and you had planned on eating a bowl of cereal and catching up on your shows on TiVo®. Cooking was not on your agenda tonight, but this is the guy you're trying to impress, right? This is the perfect opportunity to kick into Get 'Em Girl mode and make it happen in the clutch.

So you run home, with an hour to work with. You put the dirty dishes in the dishwasher, make your bed, and throw your scattered clothes in the closet. Kick the shoes under the bed and run to the kitchen to see what you can whip up. There's not much, but we're sure we can make something happen with what you have.

The recipes in this section are quick, easy, and delicious. Enjoy them and HURRY UP!

Effortless *Chicken Parmesan* And *Angel Hair Pasta*

*q*uick and easy to make, but you can let him think you've been sweating in the kitchen all evening.

1 Bring a large pot of lightly salted water to a boil over high heat. Add the pasta and prepare according to package directions for al dente.

2 Heat 1/2 inch olive oil in a large frying pan over medium to medium-high heat. Season chicken tenders with salt and pepper. Place flour in a shallow dish. Beat eggs in a second dish along side the flour.

3 In a third dish, combine the bread crumbs, 1 cup of Parmesan cheese, thyme, parsley, and red pepper flakes. Coat chicken in flour, then egg, then bread crumb mixture. Cook chicken until deeply golden on each side, 4 to 5 minutes, and transfer to 8 x 8-inch baking dish.

4 Pour a little of the sauce on the chicken tenders, and bake for an additional 10 minutes, or until cooked through. Remove from oven and top with the shredded mozzarella and the 1/2 cup of Parmesan cheese. Place in the oven to melt the cheese, and remove. Coat the hot, cooked pasta lightly with sauce, top with the chicken, and serve.

MAKES 4 TO 6 SERVINGS

INGREDIENTS

1 (16-ounce) box angel hair pasta uncooked

Olive oil, for frying

1-1/2 pounds chicken breast tenders

1/4 teaspoon salt

1/4 teaspoon freshly ground black pepper

1 cup all-purpose flour

2 large eggs, lightly beaten

2 cups Italian-style bread crumbs

1 cup shredded Parmesan cheese, plus 1/2 cup

1-1/2 tablespoons dried thyme

1 cup flat-leaf parsley, chopped

1/2 teaspoon crushed red pepper flakes

Easy tomato sauce (recipe next page)

1/2 cup shredded mozzarella cheese

Easy *Tomato* *Sauce*

INGREDIENTS

**2 tablespoons
extra virgin olive oil**

1 small onion, chopped

**1 small green pepper,
seeded and chopped**
(optional)

2 garlic cloves, minced

**1 (15-ounce) can
crushed tomatoes**

1 (29-ounce) can tomato sauce

1 teaspoon dried oregano

1 teaspoon dried thyme

**1/2 teaspoon
Italian seasoning blend**

**1 tablespoon
granulated sugar** (optional)

Salt and pepper to taste

1 Add 2 tablespoons of olive oil, onions, green peppers, and garlic to a saucepan and cook over medium-low heat. Stir occasionally for 10 minutes.

2 Add both cans of tomatoes to the saucepan and bring sauce to a light boil.

3 Season with remaining ingredients, and salt and pepper, to your taste. Reduce heat and simmer for 15 minutes.

4 Use immediately, or cool completely and store in an airtight jar. Sauce will keep for up to 3 days.
MAKES ABOUT 4 CUPS

Cheddar Garlic Biscuits

*t*he garlic butter makes them so tasty! Be sure to refrigerate the leftovers (if there are any).

1 Preheat oven to 450 degrees.

2 Combine the biscuit mix, milk, and cheese in a medium bowl until a soft dough forms. Drop by the spoonful onto an ungreased baking sheet.

3 Bake until golden brown, about 8 to 10 minutes.

4 Mix the butter and garlic powder together in a small bowl. Brush over the hot biscuits. Serve immediately.

MAKES 6 TO 8 SERVINGS

INGREDIENTS

2 cups baking mix,
(recommended: Bisquick)

2/3 cup milk

1/2 cup shredded cheddar cheese

1/2 cup butter, melted

1/4 teaspoon garlic powder

Simple *Salad* With *Balsamic Vinaigrette*

INGREDIENTS

SIMPLE BALSAMIC VINAIGRETTE
1/4 cup
extra virgin olive oil

3 tablespoons
balsamic vinegar

1/2 teaspoon
granulated sugar

Salt and freshly
ground black pepper

SALAD
1 heart of romaine lettuce

6 cherry tomatoes, halved

1/2 cucumber, diced

1/4 cup red onion, diced

1 small carrot,
peeled and shredded

1 In a glass jar, combine the olive oil, balsamic vinegar, and sugar. Season to taste with salt and ground black pepper. Shake well and set aside.

2 Wash the lettuce and dry leaves well. Tear leaves into 1 to 2 inch pieces; transfer to a salad bowl.

3 Top lettuce with tomatoes, cucumber, onion, and carrot. Toss well and drizzle liberally with vinaigrette.

MAKES 2 TO 4 SERVINGS

Tiramisu
For *Two*

a creamy and delicious Get 'Em Girl twist on a classic Italian dessert.

1 In a medium bowl with an electric mixer on medium-high, beat the mascarpone cheese, 1/4 cup of the heavy cream, 1/4 cup confectioners' sugar, and liqueur until thickened

2 Arrange 3 lady fingers onto each of 2 dessert plates or custard cups. Brush each lady finger with about 1 teaspoon of the chilled coffee. Spread 1/2 of the mascarpone mixture over the lady fingers and sprinkle with 1 teaspoon of the crumbled toffee bits.

3 Layer each with another 3 lady fingers, brushing with 1 teaspoon of the chilled coffee. Spread the remaining mascarpone mixture over the lady fingers and sprinkle with 1 teaspoon toffee bits. Top with the last 3 lady fingers.

4 Beat the remaining 1/4 cup cream and confectioners' sugar in a small bowl with an electric mixer on medium-high, until soft peaks form, about 1 minute. Spread evenly over the top of the lady fingers and sprinkle with the remaining toffee bits. Refrigerate for at least 1 hour to set and blend flavors.

MAKES 2 SERVINGS

INGREDIENTS

1 cup mascarpone cheese, softened

1/2 cup heavy cream, divided

1/4 cup, plus 2 tablespoons confectioners' sugar

2 tablespoons coffee-flavored liqueur
(recommended: Kahlua)

18 lady fingers sponge cakes

2 tablespoons prepared coffee, chilled

1/4 cup crumbled chocolate-covered English toffee bits
(recommended: Heath)

Jumpin' *Jumpin'* *Jambalaya*

INGREDIENTS

3 tablespoons olive oil

8 ounces andouille sausage, sliced

1 large onion, chopped

1 medium green pepper, seeded and chopped

3 celery ribs, chopped

2 cloves garlic, chopped

1-1/2 pound shrimp, peeled and deveined

1 (16-ounce) can tomato sauce

1-1/2 teaspoons Cajun seasoning

1 teaspoon salt, plus more to taste

1/4 teaspoon freshly ground black pepper

1/4 teaspoon ground cayenne pepper (optional)

2 scallions, chopped, garnish

Cooked steamed white rice, for serving

*t*his recipe is a quick and easy way to add a little spice to an already spicy evening. Just because you're short on time, doesn't mean your food should be short on taste. Enjoy with steaming white rice and set the evening off N'Awlins style.

1 Heat the olive oil in a Dutch oven over medium-high heat. Add the sausage, onion, bell pepper, celery, and garlic; cook and stir until onion becomes translucent, about 5 minutes. Stir in the shrimp; cook and stir until shrimp turn pink.

2 Stir in remaining ingredients and cook until heated through. Serve immediately over rice and garnish with scallions.

MAKES 6 TO 8 SERVINGS

Junior's *Shepherd's Pie*

"*T*his recipe was a staple in my house while growing up. My daddy used to put his foot in it – well I put two! This is my daddy's recipe, kicked up!" *Jeniece*

1 Preheat the oven to 400 degrees.

2 Heat a large skillet over medium-high heat. Add the vegetable oil and the ground beef. Season meat with the seasoned salt and black pepper. Brown and crumble meat until fully cooked and no longer pink. Stir in the onions and cook until the onions are translucent, about 5 minutes. Using a slotted spoon, transfer beef to a bowl.

3 In a separate medium skillet, cook the butter and flour together over medium heat for 2 to 3 minutes. Gradually whisk in the broth. Bring the gravy up to a boil and then remove from heat. Season to taste with seasoned salt and black pepper.

4 Begin layering an 8 x 8-inch square casserole dish with 1 cup of mashed potatoes, all of the meat, and the peas. Spoon the gravy over the top of the casserole and top with cheddar cheese. Top with the remaining cup of potatoes, making sure to spread evenly, and sprinkle with paprika.

5 Bake in preheated oven until potatoes are evenly browned, about 7 minutes. Let stand for 5 minutes and serve.
MAKES 4 TO 6 SERVINGS

INGREDIENTS

1 tablespoon vegetable oil

1-1/2 pounds ground beef

1 teaspoon seasoned salt, plus more to taste

1/2 teaspoon freshly ground black pepper, plus more to taste

1 small onion, finely chopped

2 tablespoons butter

2 tablespoons all-purpose flour

1 cup beef broth

2 cups Pure Bliss Mashed Potatoes, recipe below

1/2 cup frozen peas, thawed

1 cup cheddar cheese, shredded

1/2 teaspoon paprika

Pure Bliss Mashed Potatoes

1 Bring a large pot of lightly salted water to a boil over high heat. *2* Slice the potatoes 1/4-inch thick and cook in the boiling water until fork tender, about 15 minutes. Drain and transfer to a large bowl. *3* Using a potato masher, mash potatoes until slightly smooth, a few lumps are fine. *4* Add milk, butter, and sour cream to the potatoes. Mash until combined and season with salt and pepper. Serve hot. **MAKES 4 TO 6 SERVINGS**

INGREDIENTS

8 medium unpeeled red bliss potatoes, washed and scrubbed

1/2 cup milk

6 tablespoons butter

1/4 cup sour cream

Salt and pepper to taste

Get 'Em Girl
Cheat Sheet

*H*ere we go ladies! You've decided you would go to a football game with your man, or you might just be watching it on the tube with him and his friends at home. Football can be very exciting while the game is in progress and during timeouts. Where else can we go to see 22 fit men running up and down a 100 yard field, tackling each other and dancing in the end zone, and, oh, ok... let's calm down! Believe us ladies, this is not just a "man's sport"; football is lots of fun for everyone that understands it.

LET'S START WITH THE BASICS:
The object of the game is just like all other games: To outscore your opponent! Players do this by advancing the football into their opponent's end zone for as many touchdowns as possible.

Make sure you get dibs on the most comfortable seat in the house because you are going to be in it for a while. Games are divided into four 15-minute quarters. There is time for a bathroom break after the second quarter; this is referred to as "halftime." Games will run well over 60 minutes, due to halftime, TV timeouts, referee calls, team timeouts, and overtime, so be prepared to spend at least two hours per game!

Unfortunately, ladies, there can only be a total of 22 succulent bodies on the field (11 players from each team) at one time. A football team is composed of an offense, a defense, and special teams. The offense is on the field when your guy's favorite team has possession of the ball. Offensive players consist of the quarterback, running backs, wide receivers, offensive linemen and tight end. The large, muscular men playing against them are called the defensive players. Their purpose is to line up and stop the offense from scoring. Defensive players consist of the cornerback, safeties, linebackers, defensive ends, and defensive tackles. Special teams participate during kicking situations (punts, field goals, and kickoffs). Special team players consist of the holder, kick returner, snapper, place kicker, punter, punt returners and gunners.

Before each game the captains of each team meet in the center of the field with the referees (those short men with white pants and black and white striped shirts) for a coin toss. Whoever wins the coin toss has the option of starting the game by kicking the ball to the other team or having the other team kick the ball to them. So basically, the game begins with a KICKOFF! When one of the teams kicks off, the receiving team must catch the ball and proceed to advance as far as possible toward the kicking team's end zone.

Pandemonium in the stands, players dancing in the end zone, or fireworks on the field can only mean one thing... TOUCHDOWN! Touchdowns are worth 6 points and are awarded when a player carries the ball or catches a pass in the opponent's end zone.

Super Bowl Sundays

SWEET & SPICY RIBS

PARTY WINGS

PIZZA BITES

VEGETABLE TEMPURA

HOT LIKE FIRE BUFFALO WINGS

SAUSAGE ROLLS

CRAB CAKES

Super Bowl Sunday

*h*is boys are on their way over to watch the game.

Do you:

A. Go in the bedroom and stay secluded until they leave?

B. Interrupt the game every five minutes to ask, "Is it over yet?"

C. Whip up some of your smoking buffalo wings with blue cheese dip, grab a cold Corona (with a slice of lime, of course), and grab a seat?

If you are a Get 'Em Girl, we know you chose "**C**".

There is absolutely nothing wrong with playing hostess to your man's friends. You get to see the type of guys he chooses to run with, all the while forming an alliance with them that may come in handy one day.

Sweet And Spicy Ribs

Add a little spice to game night with these tender, succulent ribs.

1 Preheat oven to 350 degrees.

2 Heat the olive oil in a large Dutch oven over medium-high heat. Season ribs with salt and pepper and brown on all sides. Remove from heat and set aside.

3 In a food processor, combine honey, ketchup, ginger, and chipotles with adobo sauce. Blend until smooth. Taste and add more chipotles or honey, if desired. Pour half of the sauce over the ribs and toss.

4 Place the ribs in the oven and place the lid loosely on the Dutch oven, to allow the steam to escape and the sauce to thicken.

5 Cook until the meat is very tender, about 1-1/2 to 2 hours. Remove from the oven and serve hot, with remaining sauce on the side.

MAKES 4 TO 6 SERVINGS

INGREDIENTS

2 tablespoons plus 1-1/2 teaspoons extra virgin olive oil

1 slab (about 3-pounds) baby back ribs, skin removed and separated

Salt and freshly ground black pepper

2 cups honey

2 cups ketchup

1-1/2 teaspoons dried ground ginger

1 (7-ounce) can chipotles in adobo sauce

Cookie's *Party* *Wings*

INGREDIENTS

Vegetable oil, for frying

1 pound chicken wings, tips removed

1 tablespoon seasoned salt

1-1/2 teaspoons ground black pepper

1 teaspoon onion powder

1 teaspoon garlic powder

1 packet Sazon with annatto

1/2 cup buttermilk

2 cups flour

*W*ings! The perfect meal at any party. These wings are crispy and full of flavor. Add a little ranch or blue cheese dressing, or just a bit of hot sauce and they are good to go.

1 Preheat oven to 350 degrees.

2 In a deep fryer or high-sided skillet, heat oil to 360 degrees.

3 Wash chicken wings and pat dry. In a small mixing bowl combine the seasoned salt, black pepper, onion powder, garlic powder, and Sazon. In a separate bowl combine the buttermilk, 1/2 tablespoon seasoning mixture and 1/2 cup flour. Mix well to make a paste.

4 Season chicken with 2 teaspoons of seasoning mixture. Season the remaining flour with remaining seasoning mixture. In batches, dip wings one at a time into batter, allowing excess to drip off, and dredge in flour.

5 Carefully add the chicken to the deep fryer and cook for 6 to 8 minutes, moving and turning frequently with tongs.

6 Remove chicken with a slotted spoon and drain on a paper towel-lined platter.

7 Transfer to a baking sheet and bake until crisp, about 10 minutes.

MAKES 6 TO 8 SERVINGS

Pizza Bites

Who needs delivery when you've got a Get 'Em Girl? These little bite-size pizzas are so good, your man's friends might start placing orders.

1 Preheat oven to 450 degrees.

2 Using a 3-1/2inch round cookie cutter, cut rounds from pizza dough to make 10 individual crusts. Place pizza rounds on a baking sheet, top with sauce, and cover with mozzarella. Sprinkle with Parmesan and top with your favorite topping.

3 Bake until cheese is melted, approximately 10 minutes. Serve hot.

TOPPING SUGGESTIONS: pepperoni slices, crumbled Italian sausage, or grilled chicken.

MAKES 10 PIECES

INGREDIENTS

2 large store-bought, pre-baked pizza shells
(recommended: Boboli)

2 cups Easy Tomato Sauce
(SEE RECIPE, PAGE 92)

I cup shredded mozzarella cheese

1/4 cup grated Parmesan cheese

Toppings of your choice

Vegetable Tempura

INGREDIENTS

2 cups all purpose flour

1/2 teaspoon salt

2 cups seltzer, chilled

Vegetable oil for frying

2 pounds assorted vegetables, washed and patted dry:

- Zucchini, sliced into 1/2-inch thick sticks

- Broccoli florets

- Carrots, 1/2-inch thick slices

- Cauliflower florets

for the veggie lovers, these are bite-size and delicious. Serve with the delectable Soy Dipping Sauce along side for added flavor.

1 In a large bowl, whisk together flour and salt. Slowly add 1 cup seltzer, whisking mixture until smooth. Let batter stand for 10 minutes. If necessary, thin batter with remaining seltzer, pouring in 1/4 cup at a time until you reach the consistency of thin pancake batter.

2 In a deep fryer or high-sided skillet, heat vegetable oil to 375 degrees. Working in batches, dip vegetables in batter, shaking off excess. Carefully add vegetables to the deep fryer.

3 Fry until golden brown. Remove vegetables with a slotted spoon and drain on a paper towel-lined platter. Serve immediately.
MAKES 6 TO 8 SERVINGS

INGREDIENTS

2 scallions white and green parts, sliced

2 tablespoons rice wine vinegar

1/2 cup soy sauce

1 tablespoon fresh ginger, grated

Soy Dipping Sauce

1 Combine all ingredients in a medium bowl and stir to mix well. Serve along side the Vegetable Tempura.
MAKES 4 OUNCES

Hot-Like-Fire
Buffalo Wings

*T*he ultimate game day food. These are hot, tangy, and damn good! Enjoy them with our blue cheese dressing and a cold beer to get the party started right.

1 Preheat oven to 425 degrees.

2 Wash chicken wings and pat dry. In a shallow pan, bake wings for 1 hour. Remove and set aside.

3 In a large bowl, combine pepper sauce and melted butter. Toss in chicken wings, and mix to coat thoroughly. Let sit for 5 minutes and serve.

MAKES 6 TO 8 SERVINGS

INGREDIENTS

2-1/2 pounds
chicken wings, disjointed,
with tips removed

1/2 cup hot pepper sauce

1/3 cup butter, melted

Sausage Rolls

INGREDIENTS

1 (16-ounce) package
polska kielbasa,
cut into 6 (3-inch) pieces

1 (8-ounce) can refrigerated
crescent rolls

1 egg, beaten

*T*his is a grown folks' version of "pigs-in-a-blanket." Nothing like having a house full of grown men and only cocktail franks to feed 'em—You are bound to have a problem! Add the spicy and sweet honey mustard sauce for good dipping.

1 Preheat oven to 350 degrees.

2 Roll out crescent rolls and separate into 6 pieces. Roll each piece of kielbasa in the crescent roll and place on a baking sheet. Gently brush beaten egg over the dough.

3 Bake until crescent roll is golden brown and puffed, about 15 to 20 minutes. Serve with honey mustard sauce.

MAKES 6 SERVINGS

INGREDIENTS

1-1/2 cups mayonnaise

1/4 cup prepared
Dijon-style mustard

1/2 cup honey

Honey Mustard Sauce

1 In a small bowl, combine all ingredients and stir to mix well. Transfer to a bowl and serve along side the sausage rolls.

MAKES ABOUT 2 CUPS

Crab Cakes

*b*ring the harbor to your home with these delicious lump crab cakes. Serve with classic Tartar Sauce or delicious Mango Mayo.

CRAB CAKES

1 Heat olive oil in a medium skillet over medium-high heat. Add the scallions; cook and stir until tender. Remove from heat and allow to cool.

2 Meanwhile, in a large bowl, mix together the crabmeat, cracker meal, egg, mayonnaise, dry mustard, garlic powder, crab boil seasoning, salt, and black pepper. Shape into 1/2 inch thick patties and dust with flour. Refrigerate the crab cakes on a parchment paper-lined platter for 1 hour, to allow cakes to set.

3 Heat vegetable oil in a large skillet over medium heat. In batches, carefully place crab cakes in the pan and fry until golden brown on each side, about 8 to 10 minutes. Drain briefly on a paper towel-lined platter. Serve warm with tartar sauce or mango mayo.

MAKES 4 SERVINGS

CLASSIC TARTAR SAUCE

In a small bowl, combine all ingredients and stir to mix well. Refrigerate until ready to serve.

MANGO MAYO

In a small bowl, combine all ingredients and stir to mix well. Refrigerate until ready to serve.

INGREDIENTS

CRAB CAKES

1 tablespoon olive oil

2 stalks scallions, finely chopped with tops

1/2 pound jumbo lump crabmeat

1/3 cup cracker meal, (recommended: Ritz)

1 egg, slightly beaten

1 tablespoon mayonnaise

1 teaspoon dry mustard

1/2 teaspoon garlic powder

1/4 teaspoon crab boil seasoning (recommended: Old Bay)

1 teaspoon salt

1/2 teaspoon ground black pepper

Dash cayenne pepper

Flour, for dusting

1/2 cup vegetable oil

CLASSIC TARTAR SAUCE

1 cup mayonnaise

1 tablespoon sweet pickle relish

1 tablespoon minced onion

Salt and pepper to taste

MANGO MAYO

1/2 cup mayonnaise

3 tablespoons mango nectar

1 teaspoon fresh lime juice

Salt and pepper to taste

Hot *Plate Love*

Dorm Room Passion MENU

HEARTY BLACK BEAN CHILI

CHICKEN AND BROCCOLI STIR-FRY

CHERRY GRANITA

Entry-Level Loving MENU

SHRIMP SCAMPI WITH LINGUINI AND TOASTY GARLIC BREAD

TANTALIZING TANGY MEATLOAF

LOADED SWEET POTATOES

FUDGE BROWNIE BOWL

*h*ot Plate Love is dedicated to anybody on a SERIOUS budget.
Whether you are a struggling college student, a struggling
graduate (with student loans kicking in), or if the check didn't
quite cut it this week…this one is for you!

Plan Meals: By planning your meals ahead you can make the
best use of leftovers. If Monday is spaghetti with meat sauce,
that same meat sauce can be transformed into a wonderfully
hearty chili on Tuesday – just by adding a few simple ingredients.
Freeze any of the meat sauce/chili that you don't eat in individual
freezer bags for quick meals later on in the month.

Shop Smart: Before you even think about going to the
supermarket, create a shopping list, making sure to check your
cabinets and refrigerator for ingredients you have on hand.
Next, tuck your cute little tail between your legs and get out
the scissors and Sunday paper—clip those coupons, but only
for things you need! One other thing: grab a sandwich
or protein bar to eat before hitting the supermarket. There's
nothing more expensive than going food shopping on an
empty stomach.

Don't be afraid to buy store-brand foods: Ok, there are no
cool green mascots and the labels look really, really generic;
but so what if the taste is the same, who cares? Canned corn
is canned corn—but don't fool yourself into thinking Fruity
'Oh's and Fruit Loops are one in the same. Save where you
can, but splurge a little where you need to.

Hearty *Black Bean Chili*

*t*his delicious and filling one-pot dish can be stretched further than you might imagine. Trust us — we live in New York City, remember? So even if you invite that cute Kappa you met at the library last week over for dinner, there will still be enough to last you a day or two— or three.

1 Heat the olive oil in a large pot over medium heat. Add the onions and green peppers to the pot; cook and stir until the onions are translucent, about 5 minutes. Add the ground turkey to the pot and cook until no pink shows.

2 Stir in the remaining ingredients and reduce heat to low. Cover and simmer until the flavors are well blended, about 1-1/2 to 2 hours. Serve hot over white rice or with homemade tortilla chips (recipe below).

MAKES 6 SERVINGS

INGREDIENTS

1 tablespoon olive oil

1 small onion, diced

1 small green pepper, seeded and diced

1 (2-pound) package ground turkey breast

1 (15-ounce) can black beans, undrained

1 (14.5-ounce) can crushed tomatoes

1 (8-ounce) can tomato sauce

4 tablespoons chili powder

1 teaspoon ground cumin

1 teaspoon garlic powder

1 teaspoon salt

1/2 teaspoon ground black pepper

1/8 teaspoon ground cayenne pepper

Homemade *Tortilla Chips*

1 Heat the vegetable oil in a large skillet over medium heat. Meanwhile, quarter the tortillas and separate. *2* Carefully add the tortillas to the hot oil. Fry 1 to 2 minutes per side and remove. Drain on a paper towel-lined platter. Season to taste with salt while still hot. Serve warm with your favorite salsa.

MAKES 2 TO 4 SERVINGS

INGREDIENTS

1/4 cup vegetable oil

6 small flour tortillas

Salt

Chicken And Broccoli Stir-fry

INGREDIENTS

2 (3-ounce) packages
chicken-flavored
ramen noodles

3 tablespoons margarine

1 small onion,
cut into 1-inch strips

1-1/2 cups
frozen broccoli florets,
thawed

1 small red bell pepper,
cut into 1-inch strips

1 (8-ounce) package cooked
chicken breast
(recommended: Perdue Shortcuts)

Salt and pepper

1/2 teaspoon garlic powder

1 tablespoon
all-purpose flour

1/4 cup water

1 tablespoon
low-sodium soy sauce

*C*heap eats at its best!

1 To prepare the ramen noodles, bring a large pot of water to a boil. Add noodles and cook for 3 minutes. Drain and set aside.

2 Cut chicken breast in 1/2-inch pieces. In a large skillet, melt the margarine over medium heat. Add the chicken, onion, and bell pepper to the skillet; cook and stir until onions are translucent.

3 Add the broccoli and season to taste with salt and pepper, and the garlic powder. Continue to cook for another 5 minutes, stirring occasionally.

4 In a small bowl, mix the flour and water until dissolved. Add the flour mixture and soy sauce to the skillet. Stir occasionally and let thicken, about two minutes.

5 Remove from heat and add the prepared ramen noodles, tossing to coat the noodles. Adjust seasoning with salt and pepper as necessary, and serve immediately.

MAKES 4 SERVINGS

Cherry Granita

Okay, it's just frozen Kool Aid — but doesn't it sound good?

1 In a large pitcher, combine the drink mix and water, stirring until mix is completely dissolved. Pour into an 8 x 8-inch square dish.

2 Freeze until firm, about 3 hours, removing dish from the freezer every 30 minutes to scrape with a metal spoon, leaving scrapings in the dish to harden.

3 Remove from freezer 10 minutes before serving to soften. Scoop into a bowl, garnish with a maraschino cherry, and serve immediately.

MAKES 7 (8-OUNCE) SERVINGS

INGREDIENTS

4 cups cold water

1/3 cup cherry-flavored sweetened drink mix
(recommended: Kool Aid)

Maraschino cherries

Shrimp Scampi
With *Linguini*

INGREDIENTS

1 (16-ounce) package linguini noodles, uncooked

5 tablespoons extra virgin olive oil, plus more for drizzling

5 tablespoons butter

2 shallots, finely diced

2 cloves garlic, minced

1 pound shrimp, peeled and deveined

1 teaspoon kosher salt

1/4 teaspoon freshly ground black pepper

1/4 cup dry white wine

1 teaspoon fresh lemon juice

1/4 cup fresh parsley, finely chopped

You've got your first check and your first love — splurge a little!

1 Prepare pasta according to package instructions for al dente. Drain and set aside.

2 Meanwhile, heat 3 tablespoons of olive oil and 3 tablespoons of butter in a large skillet over medium-high heat. Add the shallots and garlic to the pan; cook and stir until the shallots are translucent, about 2 to 3 minutes.

3 Season the shrimp with salt and pepper and add to the pan. Cook until they turn pink, about 2 to 3 minutes. Remove the shrimp from the pan and set aside.

4 Add the wine and lemon juice to the pan and bring to a boil. Add the remaining 2 tablespoons of butter and 2 tablespoons of olive oil. When the butter has melted, return the shrimp to the pan.

5 Remove from heat and add the parsley and cooked pasta. Toss to coat the pasta and drizzle with a bit more olive oil. Serve immediately.

MAKES 4 SERVINGS

INGREDIENTS

1 loaf Italian bread

1/2 cup butter

2 cloves garlic, minced

Toasty Garlic Bread

1 Preheat broiler. *2* Cut the Italian bread in half, lengthwise. Place butter and garlic in a large roasting pan and heat on the top of the stove until the butter melts. *3* Place bread halves cut sides up on a baking sheet and toast in the broiler until golden brown. Remove from the broiler and place in melted butter mixture, cut sides down, in the roasting pan. Move the bread around in the butter mixture to saturate the bread. *4* Remove bread, slice, and serve hot. **MAKES 4 SERVINGS**

Tantalizingly *Tangy* Meatloaf

a spicy twist on an ordinary meatloaf.

1 Preheat oven to 350 degrees.

2 Using your hands, mix together the ground beef, bread crumbs, onion, egg, seasoned salt, black pepper, and tomato sauce in a large bowl.

3 Form the mixture into a loaf and place in a shallow baking pan. Pour 1-1/2 cups of BBQ sauce over the meatloaf

4 Bake for 1-1/2 hours, basting every 15 minutes, with the pan juices or until a meat thermometer reads 160 degrees when inserted in the center of the meatloaf. Remove from oven and let sit for 5 minutes before slicing.

MAKES 6 SERVINGS

INGREDIENTS

1-1/2 pounds ground beef

1 cup plain bread crumbs

1 small onion, diced

1 egg, lightly beaten

1-1/2 teaspoons seasoned salt

1/2 teaspoon ground black pepper

1/2 cup tomato sauce

1-1/2 cups Mama Cookie's BBQ Sauce (recipe below)

Mama Cookie's BBQ Sauce

1 In a medium saucepan, over medium heat, stir together the tomato sauce, light brown sugar, vinegar, mustard, Worcestershire sauce, onion and garlic powders; bring to a boil. Cook for 1 minute, stirring constantly to avoid scorching. *2* Reduce heat to low. Cook and stir for about 15 minutes. Remove from heat and use immediately or let sauce cool completely and bottle in an airtight jar, to keep for up to 1 week. **MAKES ABOUT 2 CUPS**

INGREDIENTS

1-1/2 cups tomato sauce

3 tablespoons light brown sugar

3 tablespoons white vinegar

2 tablespoons Dijon-style mustard

2 tablespoons Worcestershire sauce

1/4 teaspoon onion powder

1/4 teaspoon garlic powder

Loaded *Sweet* *Potatoes*

INGREDIENTS

2 medium unpeeled orange-flesh sweet potatoes, washed and scrubbed

2 tablespoons light brown sugar

1/2 teaspoon ground cinnamon

4 tablespoons butter, room temperature

1 Pierce sweet potatoes all over with a fork. Place on a paper towel-lined microwave-safe plate about 1-inch apart.

2 Cook on high power for 6 to 8 minutes, turning over halfway through.

3 Meanwhile, in a small bowl, combine the brown sugar and cinnamon and set aside.

4 Remove sweet potatoes from the microwave and let stand for 5 minutes. Split lengthwise and fluff the meat of the sweet potato with a fork. Dot each one with 2 tablespoons of butter and sprinkle evenly with brown sugar mixture. Serve immediately.

MAKES 2 SERVINGS

Fudge *Brownie* *Bowl*

1 Prepare the fudge brownies according to the package directions for an 8 x 8-inch pan. Let cool completely.

2 While brownies are cooling, set ice cream out to soften. Pour the fudge topping into a microwave-safe dish, and heat in microwave for 10 seconds on high. Remove and set aside.

3 To assemble, cut brownies into 9 squares. Place two brownies in a serving bowl and spoon the hot fudge on top of the brownie squares. Arrange a scoop of softened ice cream in the middle of the two brownies and serve immediately.

MAKES 4 TO 5 SERVINGS

INGREDIENTS

I (19.8-ounce) package fudge brownie mix, prepared and baked
(recommended: Duncan Hines)

I pint vanilla ice cream

Chocolate fudge ice cream topping

Sweet Tooth

Sweet Tooth

*i*f you want to end the perfect meal correctly, you have to have something sweet to send him off with. Whether it's sweet and sticky caramel cake, or warm apple pie and homemade ice cream (yes, we said homemade – don't slouch now) you know the meal isn't complete without something sweet. We are sure you'll find a recipe or two in this section that will have his sweet tooth screaming for more.

Meet-the-Parents
Carrot Cake

*h*e invited you to his family's backyard barbeque—don't you dare go empty handed! This cake will definitely leave a good impression with those closest to him.

CAKE

1 Preheat oven to 325 degrees. Lightly butter and flour a 9 x 13-inch baking pan, tapping out the excess flour, and set aside.

2 Sift together in a large bowl, the flour, baking soda, baking powder, salt, cinnamon and allspice. Set aside. In a large bowl, using an electric mixer at high speed, beat the sugar, oil, eggs and vanilla extract until well combined, about 1 minute.

3 With the mixer turned to low speed, beat in the flour mixture, scraping down the sides of the bowl as needed. Mix until smooth. Using a wooden spoon, stir in the shredded carrots, crushed pineapple, chopped nuts, and flaked coconut. Spread evenly in the prepared pans.

4 Bake until the top springs back when pressed lightly in the center, about 35 to 40 minutes. Cool completely in the pan on a wire cake rack.

5 Once the cake is completely cooled, frost and cut into 15 individual squares.

FROSTING

1 In a medium bowl, beat the cream cheese, sugar, vanilla and almond extracts with an electric mixer on low speed until smooth.

2 Fold in the whipped topping with a plastic spatula. Spread the frosting over the top of the cake.

MAKES 15 SERVINGS

INGREDIENTS

CAKE

2 cups all-purpose flour

1-1/2 teaspoons baking soda

2 teaspoons baking powder

1 teaspoon salt

1-1/2 teaspoons ground cinnamon

1/8 teaspoon ground allspice

2 cups granulated sugar

1-1/2 cups vegetable oil

4 large eggs, room temperature

1 teaspoon vanilla extract

2-3/4 cups shredded carrots

1 (8-ounce) can crushed pineapples, drained

3/4 cup chopped walnuts

1/2 cup sweetened flaked coconut (optional)

FROSTING

1 (8-ounce) package cream cheese, room temperature

1 (16-ounce) box confectioners' sugar

1/2 teaspoon vanilla extract

1/2 teaspoon almond extract

1 (8-ounce) container frozen whipped topping, thawed

Chocolate
Toffee Trifle

INGREDIENTS

1 (18.25-ounce) package Devil's Food cake mix

2 cups heavy cream

2 tablespoons confectioners' sugar

1 teaspoon vanilla

6 (1-1/8-ounce) chocolate-covered English toffee bars, frozen (recommended: Heath Bars)

*l*ooks good and tastes even better. This simple and easy dessert is great for a get-together because it's easy to make and everyone can help themselves.

1 Prepare the cake according to package directions for a 13 x 9-inch cake. Let cool for 5 minutes in the pan, and transfer to a wire rack to cool completely. Once cool, cut into 1/2 inch cubes and set aside.

2 In a large, chilled bowl, whip cream with an electric mixer until soft peaks form. Beat in vanilla and sugar until stiff peaks form. Do not over beat, as cream will become lumpy and butter-like. Cover with plastic wrap and refrigerate until ready to use.

3 Place toffee bars in a resealable plastic bag and crush with a hammer. In a large trifle dish or glass bowl, layer in this order:
1/3 of the cake cubes
1/3 of the whipped cream
1/3 of the Heath Bars

4 Repeat layers and cover with plastic wrap. Refrigerate for at least four hours before serving.
MAKES 6 SERVINGS

MAKE IT YOUR OWN

Drizzle 1/4 cup of Kahlua Liqueur onto the cake cubes prior to layering the trifle.

SHORTCUT

Save yourself some time! If you are in a rush, or just not in the mood to whip your own cream – substitute the whipped cream ingredients for two 8-ounce packages of frozen whipped topping.

Oatmeal Cookie Cheesecake

*t*here is a story behind this cheesecake —which I think we'll save for The Get 'Em Girl's Guide to Dealing with the Salty Ex! However, this cheesecake is banging! Enjoy it with a sweet Muscat dessert wine and brush your shoulder off.

COOKIE CRUST

1 Preheat oven to 350 degrees. Generously butter a 9-inch springform pan and set aside.

2 In a large bowl, mix together the oats, flour, brown sugar, cinnamon, and salt. Add the melted butter to the oats mixture and mix well. Using your hand or the back of a large spoon, press the oat mixture evenly into the bottom and up the sides of the springform pan. Bake until golden brown, about 10 minutes. Set aside to cool while making filling.

CHEESECAKE

1 In a large bowl, using an electric mixer on low, beat together one 8-ounce package of the cream cheese, 1/2 cup of the sugar, and cornstarch. Beat mixture until creamy, about 3 minutes. Beat in the remaining 3 packages of cream cheese.

2 Increase the mixer speed to high and beat in the remaining cup of sugar and the vanilla. Beat in the eggs, one at a time, scraping down the side of the bowl with a plastic spatula, as needed. Blend in the heavy cream. Mix just enough to combine the cream, being careful not to overmix the batter. Gently spoon the cheese filling on top of the oatmeal cookie crust. Bake cheesecake until the center barely jiggles when you shake the pan; about 1 hour.

3 Turn the oven off after 1 hour and open the oven door slightly. Let the cake cool in the oven for 1 hour. Once the cake has cooled, remove and cover with plastic wrap and refrigerate until it's completely cold; at least 4 hours or overnight. Remove the sides of the springform pan. Slide the cake off the bottom of the pan onto a serving plate. Top with the apple pie filling, or fruit compote of your choice.

MAKES 12 SERVINGS

INGREDIENTS

COOKIE CRUST
1-1/2 cups quick-cooking oats (not instant or old-fashioned)

1 cup all-purpose flour

1/2 cup firmly packed brown sugar

1/2 teaspoon ground cinnamon

1/4 teaspoon salt

1/2 cup plus 2 tablespoons unsalted butter, melted

CHEESECAKE
4 (8-ounce) packages cream cheese, room temperature

1-1/2 cups granulated sugar

1/4 cup cornstarch

1 tablespoon vanilla extract

3 large eggs

3/4 cup heavy cream

1 (21-ounce) can apple pie filling

Cocoa Cure
Chocolate Cake

INGREDIENTS

CAKE
1 (18.25-ounce) package Devil's Food cake

1 (3.9-ounce) package instant chocolate pudding mix

1 cup vegetable oil

1/2 cup warm water

4 eggs

1 cup sour cream

1 cup semisweet chocolate morsels

FROSTING
3 (1-ounce) squares unsweetened chocolate

1/2 cup butter

1 (1-pound) box confectioners' sugar

1/2 teaspoon vanilla extract

3/4 cup milk

*W*arning – chocolate overload! This is the chocolate cake to write home about. It is ridiculously rich and is the cure-all for those days when your man can't get it right! So call your girlfriends and break out the forks, because it's going to be a long—and delicious evening!

1 Preheat oven to 350 degrees. Grease and flour a 12-cup fluted tube pan, tapping out the excess flour, and set aside.

2 In a large bowl, using an electric mixer on high speed, beat the cake and pudding mixes, oil, and water until well combined. One at a time, beat in the eggs. Add the sour cream, scraping down the sides of the bowl, as needed. Mix until smooth. Using a wooden spoon, stir in the chocolate morsels. Spread evenly in the prepared pan.

3 Bake until the top springs back when pressed lightly in the center, about 50 to 55 minutes. Cool cake completely in pan on a wire baking rack.

4 Meanwhile, in a double boiler or in the microwave, melt chocolate and butter. In a large bowl, combine the confectioners' sugar, vanilla, and 1/4 cup of the milk. Blend in the melted chocolate mixture. Add remaining milk, a little at a time, until the frosting reaches the consistency of pancake batter.

5 Spoon the frosting into a resealable plastic bag. Squeeze the air out of the bag and close. Using a pair of scissors, snip one corner of the plastic bag and set aside.

6 Invert the cooled cake onto a cake plate and liberally drizzle the frosting onto the cake.

MAKES 12 SERVINGS

Easy *Peach* *Cobbler*

This cobbler is so damn good it comes with a matching Peachtini! If he ever needed confirmation that you are the one, this cobbler is the deal sealer. Top with a scoop of vanilla ice cream or whipped cream and invite us to the wedding!

1 Preheat oven to 350 degrees.

2 In a medium saucepan over medium-high heat, bring the peaches, 1 cup of the sugar, water, cornstarch, lemon juice, and cinnamon to a boil. Let boil for 1 minute and reduce heat to low. Simmer until the peaches are tender and the sauce starts to thicken, about 10 minutes.

3 In a deep 8-inch baking dish, melt the butter in the oven. In a medium bowl, mix the remaining 1 cup of sugar and flour. Slowly add milk to the flour mixture and stir just until combined; stir in the vanilla extract.

4 Pour the flour mixture over the melted butter. Do not stir. Spoon fruit mixture on top and slowly pour in the syrup.

5 Bake until the fruit juices are bubbling and the batter has risen to the top, creating a golden brown crust, about 35 to 40 minutes. Serve warm or at room temperature.

MAKES 6 SERVINGS

INGREDIENTS

2 cups frozen peaches, thawed

2 cups sugar, divided

3/4 cup water

1/2 tablespoon cornstarch

1 teaspoon fresh lemon juice

1/2 teaspoon ground cinnamon

8 tablespoons butter

3/4 cup self-rising flour

3/4 cup milk

1/2 teaspoon vanilla extract

Peachtini

1 Pour all ingredients in a cocktail shaker half-filled with ice cubes. Shake vigorously and strain into martini glasses.
MAKES 2 SERVINGS

INGREDIENTS

4 ounces coconut rum

4 ounces peach vodka

4 ounces ginger ale

Cream *Caramel* Cake

INGREDIENTS

CAKE
3 cups granulated sugar

1 cup unsalted butter, room temperature

6 large eggs, room temperature

2-2/3 cups all-purpose flour

1/4 teaspoon baking soda

1 teaspoon salt

1 cup sour cream

1 tablespoon vanilla extract

FROSTING
1 cup unsalted butter

2 cups light brown sugar

1/2 cup evaporated milk

1/2 teaspoon vanilla extract

1 (16-ounce) box confectioners' sugar

*M*oist, buttery caramel cake drizzled with sweet and sticky caramel. Your dentist will hate us– but your man will be sending us testimonials!

CAKE
1 Preheat oven to 350 degrees. Lightly butter and flour three 9-inch cake pans, tapping out the excess flour, and set aside.

2 In a large mixing bowl, using an electric mixer on high, cream together the sugar and butter. Beat until light and fluffy, about 3 minutes. Add the eggs one at a time, mixing well after each addition.

3 In a large bowl, sift together the flour, baking soda, and salt. Reduce mixer speed to low and slowly add the flour mixture to the sugar mixture, alternating with the sour cream. Blend in the vanilla. Pour batter evenly into the prepared pans.

4 Bake until the tops spring back when lightly pressed and a toothpick inserted into the center comes out clean, about 25 to 30 minutes. Cool in pans for 10 minutes. Carefully turn the cakes onto a wire cake rack and continue to cool completely.

FROSTING
1 Melt the butter in a medium saucepan over medium heat. Add the brown sugar and milk and bring to a boil, stirring constantly. Let boil for 2 to 3 minutes and remove from heat.

2 Combine the confectioners' sugar and vanilla in a large mixing bowl, using an electric mixer on low speed. Slowly add the brown sugar mixture and beat until smooth. Let cool slightly. If the frosting is too stiff, add a tablespoon of half-and-half or full cream to thin.

3 Spread evenly between layers and on top and sides of cooled cake.

MAKES 8 SERVINGS

Put-It-On-Him Cake

The name says it all!

CAKE

1 Preheat oven to 350 degrees. Lightly butter and flour a 9-inch fluted tube pan, tapping out the excess flour, and set aside.

2 Combine the brown sugar and cinnamon in a small bowl and set aside.

3 In a large bowl, using an electric mixer on high speed, beat the cake mix, sugar, and oil until well combined. Beat in the eggs one at a time. Add the sour cream, scraping down the sides of the bowl as needed and mix until smooth. Using a wooden spoon, stir in the pecans.

4 Pour half of the batter into the prepared pan and top with the brown sugar mixture. Spread the remaining batter evenly in the pan.

5 Bake until a toothpick inserted in the cake comes out clean; about 1 hour. Cool in pan for 10 minutes. Carefully turn the cake onto a wire rack and continue to cool completely.

GLAZE

1 In a medium bowl, whisk together the confectioners' sugar, orange juice, and vanilla extract.

2 Drizzle onto cooled cake.

MAKES 8 SERVINGS

INGREDIENTS

CAKE

2 tablespoons light brown sugar

2 teaspoons cinnamon

1 (18.25-ounce) package butter cake mix

1/2 cup granulated sugar

3/4 cup vegetable oil

4 large eggs

1 cup sour cream

1/2 cup finely chopped pecans

GLAZE

1 cup confectioners' sugar

3 tablespoons orange juice

1/2 teaspoon vanilla extract

Like-Sunshine Lemon Cake

INGREDIENTS

CAKE

2 cups all-purpose flour

2 teaspoons baking powder

1 teaspoon salt

1 cup butter,
room temperature

2 cups granulated sugar

3 eggs

Zest of 1 large lemon

1 cup heavy cream

LEMON GLAZE

1/4 cup melted butter

2 tablespoons
fresh lemon juice

2 cups sifted
confectioners' sugar

*b*righten up his day with this flavorful dessert.

CAKE

1 Preheat oven to 325 degrees. Generously butter and flour a 10-inch tube pan, tapping out the excess flour, and set aside.

2 In a large bowl, sift together the flour, baking powder, and salt; set aside.

3 Cream the butter and granulated sugar with an electric mixer on high speed, until mixture is very light and fluffy, about 5 minutes. Beat in the eggs one at a time, scraping down the side of the bowl as necessary. Blend in the lemon zest.

4 Add flour mixture to the creamed mixture, alternating with the heavy cream. Pour batter into prepared cake pan.

5 Bake until a toothpick inserted in the cake comes out clean, about 1 hour. Cool in pan for 10 minutes. Carefully turn the cake onto a wire rack and continue to cool completely.

LEMON GLAZE

1 In a medium bowl, whisk together the glaze ingredients until smooth.

2 Drizzle liberally onto cooled cake.

MAKES 10 TO 12 SERVINGS

Flaky *Pie* Crust

INGREDIENTS

1 In a medium bowl, sift the flour and salt together. Using a fork, cut the shortening into the flour until the mixture resembles small peas. Stirring with the fork, gradually add just enough of the water to make the mixture clump together. Gather up the dough and press into a thick disk.

1-1/2 cups all-purpose flour

1/2 teaspoon salt

1/2 cup vegetable shortening, chilled

1/3 cup ice water

For extra tender pie crust, do not over-work the dough. Chilling the shortening and water will help to make this piecrust flaky.

TAKE NOTE

Caramel *Appletini*

INGREDIENTS

1 Pour all ingredients in a cocktail shaker half-filled with ice cubes. Shake vigorously and strain into martini glasses..
MAKES 2 SERVINGS

4 ounces vodka

4 ounces apple schnapps

4 ounces butterscotch schnapps

Crumbly *Caramel* *Apple Pie*

INGREDIENTS

FILLING

1/2 cup packed
light brown sugar

2 tablespoons half-and-half

1/4 cup unsalted butter

1/2 teaspoon vanilla extract

I tablespoon all-purpose
flour, plus I teaspoon

5 cups peeled
Granny Smith apples,
cored and thinly sliced

1/4 teaspoon
fresh lemon juice

2/3 cup granulated sugar

3 tablespoons cornstarch

I teaspoon cinnamon

5 caramel candies, halved

CRUMB TOPPING

1/3 cup granulated sugar

3/4 cup all-purpose flour

6 tablespoons unsalted
butter, chilled

*a*ll-American? We think not! All Get 'Em Girl! Another signature dessert that comes with a matching martini — that will have him begging for more.

(FLAKY PIE CRUST & CARAMEL APPLETINI RECIPES ON PAGE 129)

1 Preheat oven to 350 degrees.

2 In a small saucepan over medium heat, cook and stir the brown sugar and the half-and-half until sugar dissolves. Remove from heat. Add the butter, vanilla, and 1 tablespoon of flour, stir until the butter melts. Set aside to cool.

3 On a lightly floured work surface, roll out the disk of piecrust dough into a 13-inch round, about 1/8 inch thick. Fold the dough in half. Transfer to a 9-inch pie pan and gently unfold it to fit into the pan. Sprinkle the bottom of the dough with 1 teaspoon of flour.

4 In a large bowl, toss the apples with the lemon juice. Add 2/3 cup granulated sugar, cornstarch, cinnamon, and the caramels. Toss to coat the apples. Spoon the apple mixture into the pie pan. Pour the cooled brown sugar sauce over the apples.

5 In a medium bowl, mix 1/3 cup sugar with 3/4 cup flour. Using a fork, cut the chilled butter into the flour mixture until crumbly. Spoon the crumb topping over the apples, making sure to completely cover them. Using a knife or scissors, trim the edges of the bottom pie crust so it hangs over just about 1 inch. Fold the dough under itself so the edge of the fold is flush with the edge of the pie pan. Crimp the crust around the edges of the pan with a fork.

6 Cover pie with aluminum foil and place on a baking sheet. Bake for 25 minutes. Remove foil and bake until golden brown and the juices are bubbling, about 20 to 25 minutes. Cool completely on a wire rack.

MAKES 8 SERVINGS

Just *Peachy*
Bread Pudding

BREAD PUDDING

1 Preheat the oven to 325 degrees. Lightly butter a 2-1/2 quart baking dish and set aside.

2 In a medium saucepan over medium-low heat, bring the peaches and peach nectar to a simmer. Cook until peaches are tender, about 5 minutes.

3 In a large bowl, gently toss the bread, 3 tablespoons melted butter, raisins, and peaches, until the bread is completely coated. In a separate bowl, whisk together the eggs, granulated sugar, half-and-half, and 1 teaspoon vanilla extract. Add the bread mixture, and mix gently. Pour into prepared dish.

4 Bake until golden brown and the center is set, about 1 hour.

BROWN SUGAR VANILLA SAUCE

1 In a small saucepan, over medium heat, combine all ingredients. Bring to a boil, stirring frequently. Reduce heat to medium-low and let cook for 5 minutes, stirring continually. Remove from heat. Sauce will thicken as it cools. Drizzle over the top of bread pudding and serve warm or at room temperature.

MAKES 4 TO 6 SERVINGS

INGREDIENTS

BREAD PUDDING
2-1/2 cups
peeled peaches,
diced (fresh or frozen)

1/4 cup peach nectar

4 cups brioche,
crust removed,
and cut into 1-inch cubes
3 tablespoons
unsalted butter, melted

1/2 cup golden raisins

3 large eggs

1/2 cup granulated sugar

1 teaspoon cinnamon

1-3/4 cups half-and-half

1 teaspoon vanilla extract

BROWN SUGAR VANILLA SAUCE
1/2 cup brown sugar

2 tablespoons light corn syrup
(recommended: Karo)

1/4 cup unsalted butter

1/2 cup heavy cream

1-1/2 teaspoons vanilla extract

Food Labels Made Easy

*t*he labels found on food in the grocery stores can be very confusing. Here we break down the facts so you can make better food choices when shopping and eating.

1. **SERVING SIZE:** This is a key piece of information when you are watching your portions. If you eat more than the serving size, the nutritional value changes as well.

2. **CALORIES:** Educate yourself on how many calories you should be eating on a regular basis. This information will help you when trying to lose weight by adopting a reduced-calorie meal plan.

3. **TOTAL FAT:** If it sounds like trouble, it may or may not be! There are bad fats (fats that raise LDL cholesterol and promote heart disease) and good fats (fats that don't raise, and may even lower LDL cholesterol). Moderate intake of all types of fat is best, to maintain a well-balanced diet. **SATURATED FAT:** This is the main dietary cause of high blood cholesterol and should be limited to 7% of your total daily calorie intake. **TRANS FAT:** Found mostly in fast foods, margarine, beef, white breads, shortenings, and store-bought cookies. It is believed to raise cholesterol levels more than saturated fats. Look for foods labeled "trans-fat free" when possible. **POLYUNSATURATED AND MONOUNSATURATED FAT:** Found in olive, canola, sesame, and corn oils, these fats may help lower your blood cholesterol level when used in place of saturated fats.

4. **SODIUM:** The recommended dietary intake for sodium is 2400 – 3000 mg per day, but if you're watching your blood pressure, or if you are suffering from high blood pressure, we suggest consuming a little less.

5. **TOTAL CARBOHYDRATE:** When reading labels, make sure you look at the total grams of carbohydrates, instead of just the grams of sugar. Carbohydrates comprise starches and dietary fiber, as well as sugar – so ready carefully.

Nutrition Facts

Serving Size 1 cup (228g)
Servings Per Container 2

Amount Per Serving

Calories 250   Calories from Fat 110

	% Daily Value*
Total Fat 12g	18%
Saturated Fat 3g	15%
Trans Fat 3g	
Cholesterol 30mg	10%
Sodium 470mg	20%
Potassium 700mg	20%
Total Carbohydrate 31g	10%
Dietary Fiber 0g	0%
Sugars 5g	
Protein 5g	

Vitamin A	4%
Vitamin C	2%
Calcium	20%
Iron	4%

* Percent Daily Values are based on a 2,000 calorie diet. Your Daily Values may be higher or lower depending on your calorie needs.

		Calories:	2,000	2,500
Total Fat	Less than		65g	80g
Sat Fat	Less than		20g	25g
Cholesterol	Less than		300mg	300mg
Sodium	Less than		2,400mg	2,400mg
Total Carbohydrate			300g	375g
Dietary Fiber			25g	30g

In *Love* 'N *Health*

My Suga's Got Sugar! MENU
GRILLED GARLIC STEAK
SMOTHERED PORK CHOPS
PERFECTLY BAKED BROWN RICE
CANDIED CARROTS
MIXED BERRY PARFAIT

What Do You Mean No More Meat? MENU
TEMPEH CHILI
KIRSTEN'S VEGGIE LASAGNA
TAWANDA'S VEGAN CARROT CAKE

Baby, I Don't Care What The Dr. Says, Your Keg is Sexy! MENU
OVEN FRIED FLOUNDER
SWEET POTATO FRIES
"SPAGHETTI" AND MEAT SAUCE
YES, THEY'RE GOOD FOR YOU OATMEAL COOKIES

*n*ow that you have found the man of your dreams and you have resolved that he is the Ossie to your Ruby, you want him around as long as possible. Whether you're pushing him out the door for personal training sessions, or working out together in the park, the key to good health is a balance of exercise and proper diet. Since the two of you are madly in love, we are pretty sure you're getting in more than enough exercise (wink), so let us take care of the food. We don't think you should forfeit taste to make the dishes healthful, so we came up with some delicious and healthful meals that you and your partner will love!

For the most part, the dishes highlighted in this chapter fall under one of three categories: low-fat, low-carb/sugar, or meat-free; so feel free to pick and choose from each section to come up with a meal your sweetie won't believe could actually be good for him.

Grilled *Garlic* *Steak*

*i*t is all about the marinade with this steak. The longer you let it marinate, the better it will taste.

1 In a small bowl, mix olive oil, soy sauce, vinegar, ketchup and garlic. Place flank steak in a large resealable plastic bag. Pour marinade over steak.   Seal and refrigerate for at least 3 hours.

2 Heat a grill pan over medium-high heat. Place steak on the grill and discard marinade. Cook for 5 minutes on each side for medium-rare. Remove from heat and let rest for 3 minutes, allowing juices to redistribute.

3 Slice the steak into 1/4 inch thick strips, against the grain of the meat, before serving.

MAKES 4 SERVINGS

INGREDIENTS

1/4 cup
extra virgin olive oil

1/4 cup
low-sodium soy sauce

4-1/2 teaspoons distilled
white vinegar

2 tablespoons ketchup

2 tablespoons garlic,
chopped

1-1/2 pound
flank or sirloin steak

Smothered Chops

INGREDIENTS

4 turkey or pork chops,
1/2-inch thick

1/2 teaspoon salt

1/2 teaspoon
ground black pepper

4 tablespoons self-rising
flour (for dredging)

1/3 cup canola oil

1 medium onion, chopped

2 cloves garlic, chopped

1/2 cup chopped green pepper

1/2 cup chopped tomato

1/2 teaspoon fresh ginger,
peeled and grated

1 teaspoon fresh thyme,
stems removed

2 tablespoons
low-sodium soy sauce

1 chicken bouillon cube,
dissolved in 1/3 cup water

a diabetic-friendly variation to our suffocated pork chops — and they are just as good.

1 Season chops with salt and pepper, then lightly dredge in flour and set aside.

2 Heat canola oil in a large skillet over medium heat. Carefully add the chops to the skillet and fry 6 to 7 minutes on each side, until lightly browned.

3 Stir in the onion, garlic, bell pepper, tomato, ginger, thyme, soy sauce, and bouillon mixture. Reduce heat to low and cover; let simmer until chops are cooked through and tender, about 25 to 30 minutes. Remove from heat and serve hot with Perfectly Baked Brown Rice (below).

MAKES 2 TO 4 SERVINGS

INGREDIENTS

1 cup brown rice

2 cups water

1 tablespoon unsalted
butter (optional)

1 teaspoon salt

1/4 teaspoon freshly
ground black pepper

Perfectly Baked Brown Rice

1 Preheat oven to 375 degrees. Place the rice in an 8-inch glass baking dish. In a medium saucepan, bring the water, butter, salt, and pepper to a boil. Once the water begins to boil, remove from heat and pour over the rice. *2* Stir to combine and cover the dish tightly with aluminum foil. Bake on the middle rack for 1 hour. Remove from oven and fluff rice with a fork. Serve hot.
MAKES 4 TO 6 SERVINGS

Candied Carrots

1 Over medium-high heat, place carrots in a pot of lightly salted water and bring to a boil. Reduce heat to medium-low and simmer for 15 to 20 minutes, making sure not to overcook.

2 Drain carrots, reduce heat to low, and return carrots to the pot. Stir in the butter, Splenda® Brown Sugar Blend, salt and pepper. Cook carrots until sugar is bubbly, about 3 to 5 minutes. Remove from heat and let stand for 2 minutes; serve hot.

MAKES 2 TO 4 SERVINGS

INGREDIENTS

1 pound baby carrots

2 tablespoons butter, melted

2 tablespoons Splenda® Brown Sugar Blend

Salt and pepper to taste

Mixed *Berry*
Parfait

INGREDIENTS

2 (8-ounce) containers
plain yogurt

2 teaspoons Splenda®
granular sweetener

2 tablespoons plus
1-1/2 teaspoons
low-fat granola

1 (10-ounce) package
frozen mixed berries,
thawed

*t*his is a quick and easy way to complete any meal with
the light taste of sweet berries. You can use fresh seasonal
berries or frozen ones, whatever works for you.

1 In a small bowl, mix the yogurt and Splenda® granular
sweetener until well combined. Cover the bottoms of two
small glasses with a layer of yogurt. Cover the yogurt with 1/2
tablespoon of granola and top with the berries.

2 Repeat layers, ending with berries, until both glasses are
full. Sprinkle top with granola and serve immediately.

MAKES 2 SERVINGS

Tempeh Chili

1 Heat the vegetable oil in a large saucepan over medium heat. Add the Tempeh to the pan; cook and stir until lightly browned, about 10 minutes.

2 Reduce heat to low and add the onion, beans, tomatoes, tomato sauce, chili powder, cumin, and garlic powder. Simmer for 20 minutes and remove from heat. Serve immediately over rice

MAKES 6 SERVINGS

TAKE NOTE

What is Tempeh?

Tempeh is a fermented food made from soybeans. Unlike tofu, tempeh is made from the whole soybean and contains a high protein, dietary fiber, and vitamin content. It has the texture, appearance, and consistency of meat which makes it great for a vegetarian Bolognese sauce, stews, and other "meat" based vegetarian dishes.

INGREDIENTS

2 tablespoons vegetable oil

1 (8-ounce) package Tempeh, crumbled

1 large onion, diced

1 (8-ounce) can red kidney beans, rinsed and drained

1 (8-ounce) can whole peeled tomatoes, hand-crushed

1-1/2 cups tomato sauce

1/4 cup chili powder

1 teaspoon cumin

1 teaspoon garlic powder

2 cups hot cooked rice

Kirsten's *Vegetable Lasagna*

INGREDIENTS

1 (9-ounce) box uncooked lasagna noodles
(recommended: Barilla No-Boil Lasagne

2 large eggs

1 (15-ounce) container ricotta cheese

4 cups shredded mozzarella cheese

1/2 cup grated Parmesan cheese

Salt and pepper

3 tablespoons olive oil

1 small onion, finely diced

2 cloves garlic, minced

1 pound frozen spinach, thawed

*f*resh vegetables, layered with stringy mozzarella and ricotta cheese.
(EASY TOMATO RECIPE ON PAGE 92)

1 Preheat oven to 375 degrees. Spray a 13 x 9 x 3-inch deep lasagna pan with non-stick cooking spray.

2 In a medium bowl, beat eggs. Stir in ricotta, 2 cups of mozzarella and the Parmesan. Season with salt and pepper. Add the olive oil to a large skillet over medium-high heat. Add the onions and garlic; cook and stir until the onions are translucent, about 5 minutes.

3 Place the spinach in a colander and squeeze until all the liquid is out of spinach. Add the spinach to the pan and toss to coat. Cook and stir for 2 minutes and remove from heat. Season to taste with salt and pepper.

4 To assemble: start with a thin layer of sauce on the bottom of the lasagna pan, about 1/2 cup. Layer with 4 uncooked lasagna noodles (slightly overlapping if necessary). Next, add 1/3 of ricotta cheese mixture, 1/3 of the sautéed spinach mixture and 1 cup of sauce. Repeat with two more layers of noodles, ricotta cheese mixture, spinach, and sauce. Finish with a layer of noodles and spread with sauce. Cover with aluminum foil.

5 Bake until the sauce begins to bubble around the edges of the lasagna and the noodles are tender, about 45 minutes. Remove from oven and let rest for 10 minutes. Serve with a Quick Side Salad (recipe on page 86).
MAKES 6 TO 8 SERVINGS

Tawanda's *Vegan Carrot Cake*
With *Faux Cream Cheese Frosting*

CAKE

1 Preheat oven to 350 degrees. Grease and flour two 10-inch cake pans and set aside.

2 In a medium bowl, sift the flour, baking soda, salt, cinnamon and allspice together and set aside.

3 In a separate bowl, mix the brown sugar and shredded carrots. Cover with plastic wrap and set aside for 1 hour.

4 In a large bowl, using an electric mixer on high speed, beat the egg replacement until light. Gradually beat in the cane sugar, vegetable and coconut oils, and vanilla extract until well combined.

5 Reduce mixer speed to low, and beat in the flour mixture, scraping down the sides of the bowl as needed. Mix just until smooth. Using a wooden spoon, stir in the shredded carrot mixture. Spread batter evenly in the prepared pans.

6 Bake until the top springs back when pressed lightly in the center, about 45 to 50 minutes. Cool for 10 minutes and remove from pan. Cool completely on a wire rack.

FROSTING

1 In a medium bowl, using an electric mixer, beat the vegan cream cheese and margarine until smooth. Add the vanilla extract and confectioners' sugar and continue to beat until smooth. Spread the frosting over the top and sides of the cake.

MAKES 10 TO 12 SERVINGS

INGREDIENTS

CAKE

3 cups all-purpose flour

2 teaspoons baking soda

1 teaspoon salt

1 teaspoon ground cinnamon

2 teaspoons ground allspice

1 cup vegan light brown cane sugar

6 cups shredded carrots

3-egg equivalent of vegan egg replacer (recommended: Ener-G)

1 cup vegan cane sugar

1/2 cup vegetable oil

1/2 cup coconut oil

2 teaspoons vanilla extract

FROSTING

1 package (8-ounce), vegan cream cheese, room temperature

1/3 cup vegan soy margarine, room temperature (recommended: Earth Balance)

1 teaspoon vanilla extract

2 cups vegan confectioners' sugar

Oven-Fried Flounder

INGREDIENTS

1/2 cup fat-free milk

1/2 teaspoon salt

1/2 cup yellow cornmeal

3 tablespoons
plain dried breadcrumbs

1/2 teaspoon seasoned salt

1/8 teaspoon
ground black pepper

1/4 teaspoon paprika

1/8 teaspoon
cayenne pepper

4 flounder fillets
(about 4 ounces each)

1 tablespoon
unsalted butter, melted

*G*ive your frying pan a break and try this light and crispy dish. Make it a heart-healthy fish and chips meal with Sweet Potato Fries.

1 Preheat oven to 500 degrees. Spray a broiler pan with non-stick cooking spray.

2 In a shallow dish, mix the milk and salt, and set aside. In a separate bowl, combine the cornmeal, breadcrumbs, seasoned salt, black pepper, paprika and cayenne pepper. Dip the fish fillets in the milk and then roll in the cornmeal mixture.

3 Place the fish in the prepared baking dish. Pour the melted butter over the fish and bake 10 to 15 minutes or until the fish flakes easily when tested with a fork.

MAKES 4 SERVINGS

INGREDIENTS

4 small unpeeled sweet
potatoes, washed and scrubbed

1 tablespoon unsalted butter

1/4 teaspoon seasoned salt

1/8 teaspoon
ground black pepper

Dash ground nutmeg

Sweet Potato Fries

1 Preheat oven to 450 degrees. Spray a baking pan with non-stick spray. *2* On a cutting board, cut the sweet potatoes lengthwise, into quarters, then cut each quarter into 2 wedges, lengthwise. Arrange potatoes in a single layer in prepared baking pan. *3* In a small saucepan, over medium heat, melt the butter, then add the salt, pepper, and nutmeg. Brush mixture onto potatoes. Bake for 20 minutes or until brown and tender.

MAKES 4 SERVINGS

"Spaghetti" With Meat Sauce

Substitute pasta with spaghetti squash for a low-carb comfort food that will have him fueled and fit in no time.

1 Heat the olive oil in a large saucepan, over medium heat. Add the ground turkey, onions, green peppers, garlic, and mushrooms. Cook until brown. Do not drain.

2 Stir in the tomatoes, tomato paste, thyme, Italian seasoning blend, and oregano. Bring to a boil. Add the red pepper flakes and Splenda® granular sweetener. Reduce heat to low and simmer for 1 hour.

3 Meanwhile, bring a large stock pot of lightly salted water to a boil. On a cutting board, slice squash in half lengthwise. Scoop out the seeds with a spoon. Completely submerge both halves in boiling water and cook until the inside is fork tender and pulls apart into strands, about 15 to 20 minutes.

4 Remove the squash from the pot; drain and cool with cold water. Using a fork, scrape the cooked squash out of its skin, fluffing and separating into spaghetti-like strands. Discard the skin. Drizzle with olive oil and season with salt and pepper.

5 Spoon the meat sauce over the spaghetti squash and serve immediately.

MAKES 4 SERVINGS

INGREDIENTS

2 tablespoons extra virgin olive oil, plus more for drizzling

1 pound ground turkey

1/4 cup chopped onion

1/4 cup chopped green pepper

1 clove garlic, chopped

1/2 cup crimini mushrooms, sliced

2 (15-ounce) cans stewed tomatoes

1 tablespoon tomato paste

1 tablespoon dried thyme

1 tablespoon Italian seasoning blend

**1 tablespoon dried oregano
Dash red pepper flakes**

2 teaspoons Splenda® granular sweetener, optional

1 medium Spaghetti squash

salt and pepper

Yes-They're-Good-for-You
Oatmeal Cookies

INGREDIENTS

1/4 cup unsalted butter

1 cup Splenda®
Brown Sugar Blend

2 large eggs

1/2 cup
unsweetened applesauce

2 cups whole wheat flour

1 teaspoon salt

1 teaspoon
ground cinnamon

1 teaspoon baking soda

2 cups quick-cooking oats

1 cup raisins

2 teaspoons vanilla extract

a delicious and healthful version of the traditional oatmeal cookie. With the addition of applesauce, this is an extremely moist and almost cake-like cookie.

1 Preheat oven to 350 degrees. Butter a cookie sheet and set aside.

2 Beat the butter and Splenda® Brown Sugar Blend in a large bowl with an electric mixer until creamy. Add the eggs and mix well. With a large spoon, mix in the applesauce until well combined.

3 In a separate bowl, sift together the flour, salt, cinnamon, and baking soda. Add the oats and the flour mixture into the applesauce mixture and mix well. Fold in the raisins and the vanilla extract.

4 Drop by rounded teaspoons onto the prepared cookie sheet. Bake for 10 to 12 minutes. Remove from oven and let cool completely on a wire cake rack before serving.

MAKES ABOUT 2 DOZEN COOKIES

You Got Him...
Now What

*I*f this was a perfect world, all the ills of a relationship would be solved with the whiff of freshly baked peach cobbler. Unfortunately, this is not a perfect world and relationships require more than a banging cobbler recipe. In fact, relationships take quite a bit of work, but anything worth having is worth working for.

So, while you are putting in work in the kitchen, don't forget to keep the relationship fun, fresh, and sexy. Just in case you need a little help (which we are sure you don't) here are a few tips to guide you:

ISSUE: Against your parent's advice, the two of you decided to get an apartment together. The once sex-filled nights (and mornings) have suddenly turned into reality...and it bites! You realize quickly that love is so much sexier when you are not picking up his dirty socks from the living room floor.

ANSWER: Spice things up! Toss your good-girl image to the wind and let him know you are not to be played with! Turn your love nest into an erotic red-light district, complete with a removable dance pole (we would give you the web address...but we can't be held responsible if you break your neck!) and fare easily devoured off of or drizzled deliciously on you. If nothing else, we bet he will be picking up behind himself in no time.

ISSUE: You just got the promotion of your dreams; the corner office is to die for, the stock options are orgasmic, and the salary is...well let's just say, your Hot Plate Love days are over. Unfortunately, like the saying goes "with great power, comes great responsibility"...and your relationship is suffering. Your man hasn't seen you in a week and he is wondering if you forgot about him...even your Shih Tzu thought you were an intruder and went Cujo on your butt; what do you do?

ANSWER: Play Hooky! Wake up early and start by treating your love (and your dog) to breakfast in bed – don't forget the mimosas, you're not going to work today! Turn off your Blackberry – wait, just put it on vibrate…and treat him to a day planned just for him. Whether it's a picnic for two or a trip to his favorite bookstore…make sure it's something that he likes and is interested in. Enjoy him for the entire day, without interruption, and let him know that your career is not the only priority in your life.

ISSUE: You are tired! Food is what you need, but cooking is the last thing on your mind. Guess who just called asking "what's for dinner, baby?"

ANSWER: Take a deep breath – now let your fingers get to dialing! Hey, even Get 'Em Girl's do take out every now and then. Let him know you will order the pizza and fix the salad while he can pick the wine and movie. Keep it simple, don't sweat it, and even if you didn't make it…you can still work it.

ISSUE: The two of you have been on a relationship whirlwind for the past three-months, nothing else matters in the world except the two of you…and then, he asks you to meet his friends. You've heard all the stories about Mark's college days as a stripper and Derrick's insane ex-girlfriend crashing every event he attends – in fact, I'm sure you even confided in him some stories about your girlfriends that you are praying to God he doesn't mention in their presence, how do you handle it?

ANSWER: Make it a party! The late great Notorious B.I.G. said it best "tell your friends, to get with my friends – we can all be friends…" and you know if there's any time to show off your new culinary skills – now is the time! Keep it simple and invite your closest friends, the one's whose opinions matter the most to you, and you know won't act a straight fool when they meet your sweetie. Just be yourself, keep the menu simple, and the pillow-talk you both shared to yourselves and we are sure everything will turn out fine.

Get 'Em Girl

Index

d